# The Complete Idiot's Reference Card

## The Alphabet

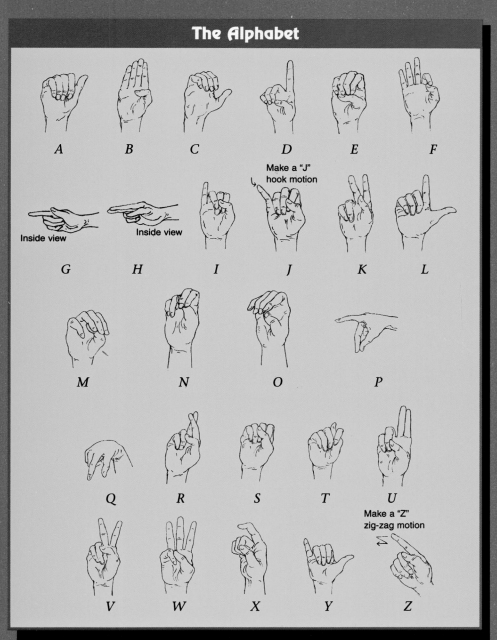

alpha
books

# The Numbers From 1–10

One.

Two.

Three.

Four.

Five.

Six.

Seven.

Eight.

Nine.

Ten.

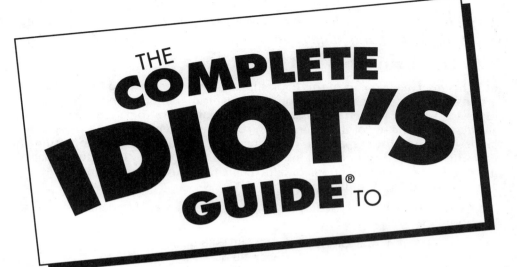

# THE COMPLETE IDIOT'S GUIDE® TO

# Learning Sign Language

*by Susan Shelly and Jim Schneck*

alpha
books

A Pearson Education Company

*To the brave, Deaf children who kept on signing through the age of oralism, despite the taunts and punishments to which they were subjected.*

## ©1998 by Susan Shelly and Jim Schneck

THE COMPLETE IDIOT'S GUIDE TO and Design are registered trademarks of Pearson Education, Inc.

International Standard Book Number: 0-02-862388-6
Library of Congress Catalog Card Number: 98-85701

03   02       8   7   6

Interpretation of the printing code: the rightmost number of the first series of numbers is the year of the book's printing; the rightmost number of the second series of numbers is the number of the book's printing. For example, a printing code of 98-1 shows that the first printing occurred in 1998.

*Printed in the United States of America*

**Note:** This publication contains the opinions and ideas of its author. It is intended to provide helpful and informative material on the subject matter covered. It is sold with the understanding that the author and publisher are not engaged in rendering professional services in the book. If the reader requires personal assistance or advice, a competent professional should be consulted.

# ALPHA DEVELOPMENT TEAM

**Publisher**
*Kathy Nebenhaus*

**Editorial Director**
*Gary M. Krebs*

**Managing Editor**
*Bob Shuman*

**Marketing Brand Manager**
*Felice Primeau*

**Senior Editor**
*Nancy Mikhail*

**Development Editors**
*Phil Kitchel*
*Jennifer Perillo*
*Amy Zavatto*

**Assistant Editor**
*Maureen Horn*

# PRODUCTION TEAM

**Development Editor**
*Nancy Warner*

**Production Editor**
*Robyn Burnett*

**Copy Editor**
*Lynn Northrup*

**Cover Designer**
*Mike Freeland*

**Photo Editor**
*Richard H. Fox*

**Illustrator**
*Jody P. Schaeffer*

**Designer**
*Dan Armstrong*

**Indexer**
*Nadia Ibrahim*

**Layout/Proofreading**
*Angela Calvert*
*Megan Wade*

# Contents at a Glance

# Contents

# Foreword

It has only been during the last couple of decades that American Sign Language, Deaf Studies, and interpreter training programs have emerged as academic professions on the college/university level. More recently, some high schools are offering American Sign Language as a language option in their curriculum. It is also exciting to see that even the elementary and middle schools incorporate some unit studies on American Sign Language, the Deaf community, and its culture.

With more Deaf children being mainstreamed in the regular classrooms and Deaf people at large being able to access more services and programs through the use of interpreters everywhere, more hearing people have become exposed to the Deaf community and their language: American Sign Language (ASL). This kind of public exposure and the resulting media coverage have stirred up increasing curiosity among hearing adults and children about the silent, intriguing language and world of Deaf people.

As a CODA (Child of Deaf Adults) and as a professional academician who has been involved in training students in American Sign Language and interpreting for almost three decades, I have witnessed the explosion of information regarding Deaf people, their culture, American Sign Language, and the profession of interpreting. Much of what still exists today (though to an increasingly lesser degree) are the hurdles that Deaf people need to overcome surrounding language barrier issues. It's incredible to think that sign language was unacceptable at one time, but is now being embraced and even given official recognition through legislation in an increasing number of states. This in itself is a major milestone. Giving credence to American Sign Language places it on an equal par with languages of other cultures—and essentially implies acceptance of the Deaf community at large.

I am pleased to be able to say that I personally know one of the authors, Jim Schneck. My friendship with Jim took root when he was still a high school student learning American Sign Language and was under the tutelage of my Deaf mother, Carrie Belle Dixon. Through the years, I have had the opportunity to work professionally with Jim in the Deaf community, as interpreters, and as colleagues on the university level, training students to learn ASL or become interpreters. Jim is one of those rare, special people who have committed his life to the mission of working with the Deaf mainstream in their struggle for education, individual rights, and accessibility.

If you are one of those people who have always wanted to learn American Sign Language, this book will help you embark on such a journey. Unlike other texts that only contain the bare presentation of signs, the authors of this book have provided you with practical information that is vital and basic to understanding how to communicate with Deaf people.

There is more than just learning signs. This book touches on topics that provide background and an understanding of the Deaf community, their language, and culture. The authors share real life experiences, both humorous and sad, that illustrate the struggles and encounters Deaf people face in the hearing community.

If you are serious about learning to sign, and becoming acquainted with the community and culture of Deaf people, this book will provide you with the basic knowledge and resources you will need.

—Karen B. Turner, D. Min.
   Associate Professor
   American Sign Language Interpreting and Transliterating Degree Program
   The University of Akron

Dr. Karen B. Turner is associate professor and founder of the American Sign Language Interpreting and Transliterating Degree Program at The University of Akron. Dr. Turner is also a CODA (Child of Deaf Adults). She was nominated for an Emmy by the National Academy of Television Arts and Sciences for Akron's Newsign television program, which holds the record for the longest interpreted news broadcast in the history of television.

# Introduction

Deaf people in this country have had a troubled, misunderstood, and overlooked history.

Largely controlled by hearing people who told them what and how to learn, how to communicate, what jobs to expect, how to raise their children, and even who to marry, Deaf people for many years accepted the labels they were given of "impaired" or "handicapped." Many Deaf people were put into institutions after they were diagnosed as mentally retarded. Some are still there. Others were cloistered in their houses and never taught to communicate. Again, some are still there. But Deaf people aren't putting up with these injustices any more. They're no longer letting themselves be labeled, and they're not letting hearing folks tell them how to live.

The Deaf Revolution started quietly, then erupted in 1988, at Gallaudet University in Washington, D.C., it continues today. Deaf people are demanding fair treatment. They are demanding to be recognized as a minority, not a group of handicapped people. They are demanding respect and dignity. They are also demanding that their language— American Sign Language (ASL)—be recognized as complete and creditable.

For years, this language of Deaf people was ridiculed and even forbidden. Children who dared to use it in school had their hands slapped and were told they were stupid. Co-author Jim Schneck remembers signing to a friend while he was in high school in Ohio. He was sternly reprimanded, while his friend was given after-school detention.

One Deaf man said he will forever associate ASL with the smell of urine, for the only place it could be used when he was in school was in the bathroom.

Now that ASL is out in the open, it is quickly being recognized and accepted as a beautiful, expressive language. Signing classes are offered through churches, Girl Scout troops, community groups, and schools; your library probably has a shelf of books on sign language; and there is even an Internet site that demonstrates ASL signs.

ASL is *the* language of Deaf people in the United States and Canada. It is not known exactly how many use it as their primary language, but it is known that ASL is finally getting the respect and admiration it deserves. You have joined a growing number of people who have chosen to learn this language. Congratulations! You're in for an interesting and rewarding adventure. Pay close attention to the material in this book that deals with deafness, the Deaf community, and Deaf culture. ASL is very closely tied with Deaf culture, and is extremely important within the Deaf community. You can't fully appreciate one without knowing something about the other.

# What You'll Find In This Book

Part 1, "Let's Start at the Very Beginning," offers lots of great background information on ASL. We'll tell you who uses it, how it's learned, and some interesting tidbits like how people in Pennsylvania giggle at the way people in Ohio sign certain words.

We'll take a look at the history of ASL and learn how hearing people tried to ban it from Deaf schools while forcing Deaf students to learn to speak English in the age of oralism. We'll give you lots of interesting information about Deaf culture, deafness and its causes, and some of the problems Deaf people face every day. And we'll tell you how to best use this book to its greatest advantage. In other words, how to get your money's worth!

Get ready to work in Part 2, "Preparing to Learn ASL." We'll tell you about the four elements of a sign and why no sign can be complete without all four. We'll cover topics such as the importance of facial expression and body language, signs that look like what they represent (iconic signs), plurals, possessives, and modified signs.

Then it's time to get busy. You're going to learn the handshapes for the American Manual Alphabet, some extra ASL handshapes, and the number handshapes. These handshapes are very important because they not only represent numbers and letters, they're used to form many other signs in ASL.

Once you've got the handshapes down, we'll move on to Part 3, "Signs You'll Need to Know." You'll really start having fun now as you learn the signs for family and friends, things in your home, jobs, schools, animals, food, and clothes. You'll learn the signs for different holidays, atmospheric conditions, directions, and geographical formations.

Each sign is carefully illustrated, with directional arrows to clarify motion. There is also a written explanation with every illustration. It's best to rely on the drawing and the written explanation, as one serves to reinforce and clarify the other.

The fun continues as we move along to Part 4, "More Signs You'll Need to Know." In this section you'll learn to sign time in seconds, minutes, hours, days, weeks, months, and years. You'll also learn the signs for the days of the week. We'll show you the signs for body parts, illnesses, and emotions, then move into colors and other descriptive signs. Signs relating to crime, law enforcement, and religion round out the section.

Just when you think you're about finished, we'll hit you with some grammar in Part 5, "Fine-Tuning." We'll talk about and give you signs for pronouns, prepositions and conjunctions, word order, questions, and negatives. Then we'll have fun looking at some of the intricacies of ASL—and some of the humor.

When you finish, you'll have a good knowledge of some common ASL signs. You'll know the basic handshapes and something about the grammar and syntax of the language. You will also have a sensitivity and understanding of the problems Deaf people have faced and why their language is so closely interwoven with their culture.

# Extras

Along the way you'll encounter bits of information that make *The Complete Idiot's Guide to Learning Sign Language* not only more readable, but more personal and relevant. In many of these shaded boxes you'll find the thoughts, recollections, and anecdotes of Deaf people, or people who work closely with Deaf people. We think you'll find these bits and pieces extremely interesting. Here's what to look for:

### Sign of the Times

These are mostly stories that in some way illustrate the chapter material they accompany, and are relevant to current ASL and Deaf issues.

### A Good Sign

These are tips or bits of upbeat information to keep you on top of every signing situation.

### Warning Sign

These are just what they say: warning signs to steer you away from mistakes, clue you in on injustices, or inform you of common misconceptions.

### Signposts

Signposts are more stories collected along the way to make the text more relevant and personal.

# Acknowledgments

The authors would like to thank the many people and agencies who provided time, information, or resources for this book. Especially, we thank the staff of Deaf and Hard-of-Hearing Services for Lancaster County and staff members at the Berks Deaf and Hard-of-Hearing Services.

Thanks also to our editors at Alpha Books: Gary M. Krebs, Nancy Warner, Robyn Burnett, and Lynn Northrup for their thoughtful suggestions and guidance. To Kim Horn, technical reviewer, for her insights and candor and, to Bert Holtje of James Peter Associates for his reassurance, knowledge and humor.

A very special thanks to artists Eva Stina Bender and Cindi Dixon, whose grace and determination sustained us in trying times, and whose personal courage inspired us. And, to Carol Turkington, a much-appreciated mentor and friend.

Finally, thanks to our families and friends, and the most special thanks to Michael, Sara, and Ryan.

# Special Thanks to the Technical Reviewer

*The Complete Idiot's Guide to Learning Sign Language* was reviewed by an expert who double-checked the accuracy of what you'll learn here, to help us ensure that this book gives you everything you need to know about learning American Sign Language. Special thanks are extended to Kim Horn.

Kim Horn is an American Sign Language teacher, Deaf advocate, and consultant. She has designed programs to assist EMS personnel in dealing with Deaf patients and accident victims. She has worked with interpreter training. She helped to found the Deaf Ministry at her church. She currently teaches ASL at a local college and serves on two boards related to disabilities services and advocacy. An avid equestrian, she lives with her husband and three children in Catlett, Virginia.

# Trademarks

All terms mentioned in this book that are known to be or are suspected of being trademarks or service marks have been appropriately capitalized. Alpha Books and Pearson Education, Inc., cannot attest to the accuracy of this information. Use of a term in this book should not be regarded as affecting the validity of any trademark or service mark. The following trademarks and service marks have been mentioned in this book:

Coke, Oldsmobile, Folgers, Heinz, *Good Housekeeping*, *Bon Appetit*, *Gourmet*, Brioni.

# Part 1
# Let's Start at the Very Beginning

*It's just a wild guess, but probably at this point you have a strong interest in, but little knowledge of, American Sign Language or ASL. Well, you've come to the right place.*

*We're going to give you all kinds of information about not only ASL, but Deaf people, Deaf culture, and lots of other interesting things relating to deafness and signed language. When you finish this section, your knowledge of this fascinating language will be nearly as great as your interest in it.*

(Hello.)

# Chapter 1

# So, You Want to Learn to Sign

## In This Chapter

➤ Learning a distinct language with its own rules and usage

➤ Defining ASL: it means different things to different people

➤ Growing acceptance of ASL

➤ Finding that ASL has distinct advantages over spoken languages

➤ Signing is only ASL

➤ Discovering how high-tech advances affect Deaf and hearing persons

American Sign Language. It's beautiful. It's controversial. And it's becoming more widely used every day. American Sign Language (ASL) is currently the third most-used language in the United States, behind English and Spanish. It is thought to be the primary language for more than half of the country's Deaf population.

But it is not only Deaf people who are learning and using ASL. Teachers, parents, and friends are embracing ASL as an effective and exciting means of communicating with those who don't hear. Its visual appeal also makes it attractive to hearing people who may not even be communicating with someone who is Deaf. ASL classes are popping up in high schools, at universities, in church halls, and at Girl Scout meetings. The language is gaining the respect and attention of people from all walks of life.

Regardless of the reason why you have chosen to learn ASL, this book will easily put you on the road to signing. You'll learn that ASL is complex in its intricate use of body language and facial expression, yet provides opportunity for simple self-expression and individuality. While this book sets goals of teaching you the basics of ASL and motivating you to learn, it also strives for an enjoyable and enlightening journey toward those goals.

# What's It All About? It Depends on Who You Ask

The definition of American Sign Language varies greatly depending on who is giving it. Technically speaking, ASL is a visual-gestural language, employed by a large percentage of the Deaf populations of the United States and Canada. It has an extensive vocabulary, its own grammatical patterns, and its own rules of usage and syntax.

Textbook definitions aside though, ASL is described in many different ways:

➤ Martin L. A. Sternberg is a Deaf faculty member at several universities and the editor of a dictionary of American Sign Language on CD-ROM. He describes ASL as "a basic and common form of language for Deaf people." The language has a vast vocabulary, he says, and can be used to express almost anything.

➤ J. Schuyler Long, head teacher at the Iowa School for the Deaf in the early part of the 1900s, described sign language as a lovely and vital means of communication between Deaf people. He says: "(Sign language) is, in the hands of its masters, a most beautiful and expressive language, for which, in their intercourse with each other and as a mean of easily and quickly reaching the minds of the Deaf, neither nature nor art has given them a satisfactory substitute."

But not everyone has been enthusiastic about sign language, and ASL in particular. It has been denounced as mere picture language and as a poor substitute for English by hearing educators who believed Deaf children should in all cases learn to speak and read lips. These educators were so adamant about the use of speech that children were punished, sometimes by having their hand tied down, for using ASL. They were told they were stupid and that speech was the *correct* language. If this sounds like something from the Dark Ages, you might be surprised to know that these things occurred as recently as 15 years ago. It was illegal—against the law—to use sign language in Ohio's public schools up until 1977, and Ohio was not unique in its banning of the language.

## Sign of the Times

Jim Schneck, who is executive director of the Deaf and Hard of Hearing Services of Lancaster County, Pennsylvania, and coauthor of this book, recalls that in 1972 he held a signed conversation with a Deaf student in a public school in Ohio. Jim was sternly reprimanded, and the Deaf student received detention for the *offense*.

Even former Miss America Heather Whitestone spoke out against ASL shortly after her coronation in Atlantic City in 1994. She called the language constraining, and said that Deaf people are not well served by using it.

"As long as they don't use English, it's not going to help them be successful," she said. Whitestone, who became Deaf at 18 months as the result of a bacterial infection, lip-reads and speaks. She also uses Signed English, which, unlike ASL, translates English word-for-word. Her reluctance to use ASL caused quite a furor. While many Deaf people applauded Whitestone's victory as Miss America, some strong proponents of ASL thought that she misrepresented Deaf people.

Jack Gannon, a special assistant to the president of the highly renowned Gallaudet University in Washington, D.C., the country's premier liberal arts college dedicated to teaching Deaf people, called Whitestone a new heroine, a star, and someone to look up to. But, MJ Bienvenue, head of the Bicultural Center in Riverview, Maryland, and a leader in the Deaf community, said Whitestone was not a suitable representative for Deaf people. "It misportrays what Deaf is," Bienvenue said.

Obviously, there are different schools of thought about what exactly ASL is and its value to Deaf and hearing persons. It is safe to say, however, that ASL is the language of choice of America's Deaf, and has become more than a language to many. To many Deaf people, ASL is a means of self-identification and a symbol of who they are.

**Warning Sign**
Here's something important to remember. Whatever ASL is, it is *not* English. Deaf people have worked long and hard to establish ASL as an independent, distinct language. Understandably, it is offensive when the language is referred to as a signed version of English. There is a signed version of English, but it is not ASL.

# A Show of Hands, Please

We've already learned that ASL is the primary language for more than half of the Deaf population of the United States. But, just how many people that includes is not entirely clear. While surveys can estimate the number of people with hearing problems, there are no definitive, recent surveys on deafness. We do know that total congenital deafness is rare. Only about one in every 1,000 babies is completely deaf at birth. But hearing loss in young children is not uncommon, sometimes due to ear infections. And hearing loss among aging people, of course, is very common.

Researchers at Gallaudet University estimate there are fewer than half a million profoundly Deaf Americans, although other studies indicate higher numbers.

It is not only those with profound hearing loss, however, who use ASL as their primary form of language. Many people with lesser degrees of hearing loss also employ ASL. Martin Sternberg reported during a 1994 interview with National Public Radio that 900,000 people used ASL as a basic and common form of language.

**Signposts**

*Profound hearing loss* indicates an inability to hear almost all sounds, generally over 90 decibels. A *decibel* is a measure of the intensity of sound, with zero being the softest and 100 the most intense.

A recent study by AT&T estimates that 22 million people in America, about 10 percent of the population, are Deaf or hard of hearing. The survey predicts that the number will continue to climb as Baby Boomers age.

It is important to realize that Deaf and hard of hearing are distinctly different conditions. Many, many people who are hard of hearing sit in front of their TVs with one hand cocked behind an ear, straining to hear the already elevated volume of the evening news or the *I Love Lucy* rerun. Most of these people are not motivated to learn sign language, only to crank up the television volume a little higher and perhaps consider a hearing aid when the excessive noise can no longer be tolerated by others in the household.

The point is, as ASL becomes more widely used, accepted, and respected, there's little doubt that more and more people with hearing problems of varying degrees will embrace it.

The shift in attitude concerning ASL during the past 20 years or so is quite remarkable. While it still is controversial and discredited by some people, ASL has found many supporters. It is not entirely clear what caused the shift in attitudes, but there are theories.

**A Good Sign**

*Sesame Street*, the Children's Television Workshop show, introduced signing to kids everywhere through its Deaf character, Linda the librarian. Linda, portrayed by the acclaimed Deaf actress Linda Bove, has been signing regularly with all her *Sesame Street* friends—both furry monsters and humans—for nearly 20 years.

The great Civil Rights movement during the 1960s drew the public's attention to the treatment of minority groups and to issues surrounding those groups. Some experts feel that Deaf people followed the lead of American blacks and started to demand respect for themselves and their language.

Linguists and researchers began exploring ASL and said publicly that it is a real language. Hearing educators were forced to look at ASL as a viable learning tool, and Deaf parents and some hearing parents of Deaf children began to insist that their children be permitted to use ASL freely. The National Theatre of the Deaf was founded and ASL began to be more commonly used in churches. Hearing people became increasingly aware of deafness and ASL, as Deaf people learned to stand up for their rights and interests.

The National Association of the Deaf became a stronger advocate for Deaf people, and the tide continued to shift.

As Deaf people became better recognized and respected as a minority, so did their language. ASL is still not accepted by everyone, but it's come a long, long way.

# ASL as a Second Language

Some high schools and colleges offer ASL as an alternative to the traditional Spanish, French, German, or Latin courses, and report that students are enthusiastic about the opportunity to learn the signed language.

An ASL teacher at a Los Angeles high school said his students are fascinated with the language. Students see sign language used on TV and are intrigued. Given the opportunity, many of them want to learn more, he said

The entire University of California system accepts ASL as a foreign language for academic credit. Among other universities that recognize ASL as a language are Harvard, Brown, Georgetown, Massachusetts Institute of Technology, and the universities of New Mexico, Massachusetts, South Florida, and Tennessee.

Some universities and colleges refuse to recognize ASL and don't allow it to be studied for credit. In most cases, however, where students have appealed this or filed complaints concerning the lack of ASL, they have won and the language has been added to the school curriculum.

# ASL in Sports

Allan Gooch, a recruiter/running back coach at the University of Central Florida in Orlando, acted like a student during the 1997 summer session and took an ASL course. The reason, he said, was so he could better communicate with a Deaf student who had been recruited to play football at UCF.

Former U.S. lightweight boxing champion Johnny Lira learned ASL so he could work more effectively with a young, Deaf boxer in whom he saw great potential. Lira said he saw that promoters were taking advantage of David Davis, who became Deaf at age 4 after a case of spinal meningitis. Lira was prompted to become his advocate, as well as his trainer.

ASL is being used more and more as it becomes widely accepted and recognized. President Clinton's major addresses are signed, as are speeches at the national political conventions and other political gatherings. The Star-Spangled Banner is signed before the start of the Super Bowl, and signers at concerts and symphonies are not uncommon. Some churches provide signing along with their spoken services, and interpreters are often found with Deaf children in schools.

**Sign of the Times**

People who had never heard of ASL got a taste of the language during the 1980s when a U.S. postage stamp featured the sign for *I Love You*. The stamp was an immediate success and raised public awareness of ASL. The *I Love You* sign is one of the best known and most popular signs.

# Poetry in Motion

Many of the benefits of ASL are obvious, but some are less tangible. First and foremost, ASL gives Deaf people an efficient means of communicating with one another and with hearing people who sign.

Signing also gives its users the opportunity to express themselves without the constraints sometimes found in speech.

Someone who is speaking might say the fish he caught was big. Then he might clarify his statement and say the fish was really big. In his efforts to impress those listening, he might say the fish was the biggest he'd ever seen, or huge, or two feet long.

A fisherman using ASL to tell the same story, however, will have an easier time of it. His body movements, facial expressions, and the intensity of his movements will convey the size of the fish with far more description and flair than the nondescript use of the words *big* or *huge*. Anyone watching a proficient signer describe the fish will know that the fish was of immense proportion.

**Warning Sign**

Because ASL is entirely visual and depends greatly on facial expression and body posture, it is imperative to keep your eyes focused on a person who is signing. Looking away from a signer, at least for anything less noteworthy than a Boeing 747 landing in the backyard, indicates a deplorable lack of interest—and of manners.

Because ASL is an evolving language, there is opportunity to fine-tune and improvise a bit. Martin Sternberg said he has observed time and time again that there is no authoritative last word on a sign. Signs are created and evolve as they are used, depending on need.

If a group of people are sitting at their computers in Phoenix, for instance, and discover they need a sign for *modem*, one of them likely would sign modem as a four-sided box attached to a telephone, Sternberg says. If the members of this group attend a computer show and discover that a Philadelphia contingent has a simpler sign for modem, they may give up the way they sign modem and adopt the Philadelphia version. Sternberg sees this as one of ASL's strengths. "It's a remarkable accommodating language. It's maybe why it's such an extremely popular language," he says.

ASL is viewed as an exciting and vibrant language, full of poetry and grace. It is fluid, not rigid, and is easily personalized by the signer.

# It Ain't the Only Game in Town

ASL is the preferred language of Deaf people in this country, but is not the only means of communication used. Indeed, it is not even the only signed language used. While this book focuses almost entirely on ASL, it would be remiss not to mention some other means of communication among Deaf people. They are listed as follows:

➤ Signing Exact English (SEE 2)

➤ Signed English

➤ Pidgin Sign English (PSE)

Until fairly recently, Signing Exact English (SEE 2) was the most widely used sign method in schools and classes for Deaf and hard-of-hearing students. It uses only one sign to represent an English word that might be represented by two, three, or even 40 signs in ASL. It uses hand signs for words, prefixes, and endings to closely emulate English.

Signed English, which is less complex than Signing Exact English, includes hand gestures signed in the same word order as English, used in conjunction with speech. While fairly easy to use, it has a limited vocabulary and can't represent the entire English language.

Pidgin Sign English (PSE) is another system of manual language, mostly used by hearing people who are learning to communicate with Deaf people. It's basically signs presented in English grammatical order. Nearly everyone using this book will probably employ PSE—with or without realizing it. Not to worry! Signers are receptive to Pidgin signing if they know you're sincere in your efforts to learn their language.

Most interpreting is done in a sophisticated form of PSE, because it is virtually impossible to translate spoken English to ASL without a time delay. What you see when you think you're watching an ASL translation probably is not true ASL, but a form of PSE. If the interpreter has memorized the script in advance, then an immediate translation from spoken English into ASL might be possible.

Teachers and linguists have not always agreed that signing is the best means of language for Deaf people. In fact, as we mentioned earlier, for much of this century, schools emphasized other methods of communication, and in some cases students were actually forbidden to use sign language.

Some alternative methods of communication, although several of these also involve some form of signing, are:

➤ Speech reading

➤ Cued speech

➤ Finger spelling

➤ Speech

Speech reading is also called lip reading (although speech reading is the preferred term). This method of communication is a way of recognizing spoken words by watching the speaker's lips. The method is seriously flawed because only between 22 and 27 percent of English sounds are visible on the lips and half of them are nearly impossible to distinguish from other sounds.

Try speech reading when someone says, "I said the scent of that had set me mad. Send it back and see that it is sent now." The words *said*, *scent*, *set*, *send*, and *sent* are homophonous, meaning they all look alike. Wow! Speech reading can also be impeded by factors such as beards, missing teeth, or mumbling.

To develop an appreciation of some of the difficulties of speech reading, stand in front of a mirror and say the following sets of words while watching your lips closely. *Grim, grip, crimp, crib*; *type, time, dime*; *beech, peach, beach*; *red, rend, read, rent, wren*. Did you get all those? Now try seeing the difference between *monkey and pig*. Surprised, huh? Now say *isle of view* and think how surprised people will be when they think they see you say, *I love you*.

Cued speech was developed in 1966 by Dr. Orin Cornett. It is essentially speech reading enhanced by explanatory gestures. The hands are used in various configurations or positions near the mouth to help the observer distinguish between similar sounds that look alike on the lips, such as *p* and *b*. Enthusiasts of cued speech say that it makes spoken language visually clear while also helping children learn a spoken language. It is an easy system to learn and generally applies to all spoken languages.

**Signposts**

If sign language were placed on a continuum, finger spelling would be at one extreme, and ASL at the other. Signed English, Signing Exact English, and Pidgin Sign English would be spread out in between.

Finger spelling is a laborious process of spelling out words by forming letters of the alphabet by various hand shapes and positions. Finger spelling is used in conjunction with ASL, primarily to identify proper nouns, brand names, etc. It is not an ideal means of communication on its own, however, because it is very slow. Even people who are very experienced in using finger spelling average only about 60 words per minute—less than half the number of words in the normal speaking rate.

Teaching speech to profoundly Deaf people has been a controversial topic for hundreds of years. While some educators feel it is not necessary for Deaf people to speak at all, others feel it is best for them to be mainstreamed. Learning speech is very difficult for nearly all Deaf people. Heather Whitestone, who was taught speech when she was a little girl, said it took her six years to learn to say her last name properly.

Lest we become too ethnocentric, we should mention that systems of manual language exist in all parts of the world. Each country has its own national sign language, but each also has different sign language dialects reflecting racial, geographical, ethnic, gender, and age differences. A sampling of countries with their own national sign language includes Australia, Belgium, Brazil, Britain, Canada (although many Canadians use ASL), China, Finland, France, Germany, Greece, India, Ireland, Israel, Italy, Japan, Mexico, Norway, Spain, and Sweden.

**Warning Sign**
There is tremendous disagreement among educators of the Deaf and Deaf people themselves when it comes to methods of communicating. So, unless you're the kind of person who enjoys bantering about political hot potatoes at the breakfast table and works into religious debates by dinner time, use caution when approaching these issues with people to whom they are relevant and important.

As you've read, ASL is by no means the only method of communication for Deaf people. It is, however, the method that is most widely used and with which the Deaf most closely identify.

# High-Tech Breakthroughs

Telecommunications devices for the Deaf, known as TDDs, were invented in the mid-1960s and became fairly widespread by the 1970s.

Robert H. Weitbrecht, a Deaf physicist and licensed ham radio operator, and James Marsters, a Deaf orthodontist, invented teletypewriters, or TTYs. These are basically visual typewriters that connect to telephone lines and enable people to type phone messages over the telephone network.

TTYs, still a very important means of communication for Deaf people, have been joined by even more sophisticated technology. Fax machines, telephone relay centers, computer modems, e-mail, pagers, and the Internet have opened doors of communication for great numbers of Deaf people.

Danny Delcambre, a Deaf businessman who owns a Seattle eatery where he is also the head chef, said technological advances have made the impossible possible in his business. He accesses voice mail to get dinner reservations and uses a local telephone relay service to order food and equipment from his suppliers.

Specially trained operators use phones with special keyboards to relay messages between Deaf and hearing customers. AT&T offers long-distance relay services in every state, and local services in 17 states with more centers planned.

### Sign of the Times

More information about AT&T's relay centers is available by calling 800-682-8786. To access an AT&T relay center, dial 800-855-2881.

Tiny computers (about the size of paperback books that can be hooked up to modems and connected with cellular phones) have been adapted for the Deaf, allowing Internet access, e-mail, and fax capabilities. These carry-along devices have advantages over standard TDD equipment because of their portability and versatility.

Fax machines and e-mail have made communicating with other Deaf or hearing persons simple. But for Deaf people, like so many others, the Internet has provided perhaps the greatest advances in communication. There are numerous Web sites dealing with Deaf issues. There are chat rooms for Deaf people, sites at which Deaf people are invited to write columns, and many others. Some of possible interest are:

➤ http://dww.deafworldweb.org—This site includes an online ASL dictionary, Deaf greeting cards, chat areas, an e-mail directory, and Deaf world news.

➤ http://www.leviworld.com—This site is a Deaf resources center that includes a business center, mailing list, information on Deaf schools, postcards, Deaf organizations, and links to other Deaf Web sites.

➤ http://www.nad.org—This site is the Web site of the National Association of the Deaf and includes news, information about conferences, and links to other Deaf Web sites.

While technology has increased opportunity for communication among Deaf people, it by no means replaces face-to-face conversation. ASL is the language used by Deaf people on the street, in schools, and at work. And it's what we're setting out to learn.

## The Least You Need to Know

➤ ASL is a language unlike any other because it has its own rules of grammar and syntax, as well as manual and non-manual gestures that make it unique.

➤ People, both Deaf and hearing, have strong views about ASL. It has been a controversial language, but is gaining acceptance and respect.

➤ It is often easier to express a thought or concept in ASL than in spoken English because of the extensive use of facial expressions and body language, and the intensity of movement.

➤ Other means of communication among Deaf people include signing exact English, signed English, speech reading, and speaking.

➤ Technological breakthroughs like TTY and the Internet help communication, but can't replace face-to-face discourse.

(Dunno.)

# Chapter 2

# Who Ever Thought of This Language?

## In This Chapter

➤ Learning the causes of Deafness

➤ Understanding that prejudice toward Deaf people is alive and well

➤ Comparing education methods in schools for Deaf students

➤ Debating over the best way to communicate

While it's well accepted that American Sign Language is a legitimate language, distinct unto itself and most definitely *not* a form of English, the origins of many of the signs are not entirely clear. We do know that ASL has been around for many years in a variety of forms—passed primarily from one generation to the next. It flourished in schools for Deaf students, despite rules forbidding the use of ASL among residents.

While ASL was evolving, educators were busy teaching Deaf students by other methods. Many misconceptions concerning Deaf people have flourished over the years, and are just now in the process of being dismantled. The Deaf are uniting and—finally—are being heard.

In this chapter, we'll look at deafness and its implications in many areas of life. We'll explore some common misconceptions concerning deafness and Deaf people, and look at how the Deaf have been seen and treated in the past. We'll also explore the roots of ASL and how it came to be the official language of America's Deaf.

# How Does Deafness Occur?

The ear is a complex organ, with intricate parts designed to work together to allow hearing. Its very complexity makes it vulnerable. Accidents, genetic disorders, disease, infection, and even noise can all damage the ear, rendering hearing loss and deafness.

No age group is immune to the risk of hearing loss. All ages, from fetus to the very elderly, are at risk of hearing loss due to various factors.

# Prenatal Causes of Hearing Loss

It is estimated that between 7 and 20 percent of Deaf and hard of hearing people suffered hearing loss due to prenatal causes. Viral disease contracted by the mother is the biggest threat to prenatal ear development, and rubella, or German measles, is the most dangerous of all the viral diseases.

Rubella can cause all kinds of problems for an unborn baby, deafness among them. About one-third of babies born to mothers who had rubella may be deaf, especially if the disease occurs within the first few months of pregnancy. Deafness can be progressive, because the virus is passed from the mother to the baby, and can remain in the baby's body after birth, causing further damage.

Rubella is especially dangerous because a pregnant woman may not even know she has it. A fever and mild rash are typical symptoms of the disease, but sometimes there are no symptoms at all. Also, a woman who gets pregnant weeks or even months after suffering from the disease can infect her unborn child because the virus may still be in her body.

Fortunately, rubella is preventable. A vaccine has been available since 1968, and some states require that a woman be tested for rubella antibodies when applying for a marriage license.

Other factors and diseases that can possibly result in deafness include cytomegalovirus (a member of the herpes virus family), syphilis, Rh factor incompatibility, cerebral palsy, loss of oxygen during birth, mumps, and the flu.

In addition to disease, certain medications can affect the hearing of an unborn child when used by the mother. The antibiotic streptomycin is known to cause hearing loss, and in rare cases the class of drugs called aminoglycosides can affect hearing. Alcohol consumed in excessive amounts by the mother during pregnancy can also affect a baby's hearing. There's more about drugs and hearing loss later in this chapter in the section "Drug-Induced Hearing Loss."

# Childhood Causes of Deafness and Hearing Loss

Almost everyone who has a child has some experience with ear infections (*otitis media*). These infections of the middle ear occur in the cavity between the eardrum and inner ear. They can be extremely painful, and tend to be worse at night when the child is lying down. In the United States, ear infections account for more than 30 million doctor visits a year. The number of hours of sleep lost (both to children and parents) because of ear infections has not been documented.

If not treated, ear infections can cause hearing loss. They used to be the single greatest cause of hearing loss, but now can be treated with antibiotics, which clears up the infection before it can damage the ear. However, temporary hearing loss might occur before treatment.

Meningitis, scarlet fever, chicken pox, encephalitis, mumps, and measles are among the other diseases that can cause hearing loss or deafness. Diseases such as typhoid fever and diphtheria used to be common causes of acquired deafness among children, but rarely occur now, thanks to immunizations.

**Warning Sign**
There are various factors that increase a child's risk of getting ear infections. A child is at greater risk if he fits one or more of these criteria: bottle-fed instead of breast-fed, male, younger than two years, living in crowded conditions, in day care, already suffering from allergies, exposed to cigarette smoke regularly, Native American, or Hispanic.

# Inherited Causes of Deafness

There are thought to be about 200 different versions of genetic hearing problems. These problems range from mild hearing loss to profound deafness. A large percentage of hearing problems that occur at birth or during a child's first few years are hereditary. Many kinds of progressive hearing problems that occur later in life are also inherited.

Autosomal recessive inheritance, in which a recessive gene for deafness is passed to a child by both parents, is the cause of between 75 and 85 percent of all hereditary deafness. If both parents have this autosomal recessive gene, their chances of having a deaf baby are one in four for each pregnancy. Most parents who carry this gene have normal hearing. Genetic testing can be done to detect the gene, but because parents who carry it usually have normal hearing, they don't typically seek testing until after the Deaf child has been born and they are considering having another child.

**Warning Sign**
Hearing problems are very often genetic, and families with members who are deaf or hard of hearing often seek genetic counseling. Such counseling explores the reasons for existing hearing loss and the implications for future generations. Many Deaf people, however, oppose such counseling, saying that seeking to limit deafness in future generations sends a clear message that the condition is considered bad or undesirable.

**Signposts**
How much noise is too much? Experts say that prolonged exposure to noise above 90 decibels is enough to damage the hair cells that line the cochlea. The roar of a motorcycle is about 90 decibels, and most rock concerts are recorded at between 80 and 100 decibels. A jackhammer has a decibel level of 120, and a jet engine is at 130, even when you're standing 100 feet away.

**A Good Sign**
The incidence of deafness caused by drugs is declining as the medical community learns more about the effects of antibiotics and other drugs. Patients, though, should always inquire about all possible side effects when using any kind of drug.

**Warning Sign**
If you ever experience tinnitus, or ringing in your ears, while taking a prescription drug, consult your doctor immediately. Tinnitus often indicates that ear damage is about to occur.

# Hearing Loss in Adults

More than 10 million adults have some degree of hearing loss. Called presbycusis, this type of sensorineural hearing loss is a natural consequence of aging. Experts say if everyone lived long enough, everyone would eventually get presbycusis.

As we age, changes occur in the hair cells within the cochlea, the spiral-shaped part of the inner ear that contains the auditory nerve endings. As a result, sound can't be transmitted as efficiently, and hearing loss, especially of high-frequency sounds, occurs.

Of course, there are other reasons for hearing loss in adults. A buildup of earwax could be responsible. There are various ear diseases, such as mastoiditis, auditory neuritis, labyrinthitis, and otosclerosis that can cause hearing loss. Hearing can also be affected by an injury to either the ear itself or the brain. Excessive noise over a period of time can result in hearing loss, too.

## Drug-Induced Hearing Loss

Former Miss America Heather Whitestone was 18 months old when she contracted a severe bacterial infection and was given two very strong antibiotics. It was known that deafness, blindness, or mental retardation were possible side effects of the medicines, but the doctors who administered the drugs deemed them necessary to save her life.

Three months after she took the drugs, it was discovered that the little girl was deaf. Her mother dropped a stack of pots and pans and Heather never flinched. Her hearing loss was attributed to the powerful antibiotics.

These drugs that affect hearing by interfering with the function of the inner ear are called ototoxic drugs. Their effects can be intensified when they're used in combination with other drugs or over long periods of time. People of all ages can be affected by these drugs. In addition to antibiotics such as those Whitestone received, drugs that can affect hearing include those derived from quinine, aspirin and salicylates, loop diuretics (drugs to prevent water retention), and some anti-cancer drugs. Substances such as tobacco, alcohol, caffeine, oral contraceptives, and carbon monoxide can also cause reactions that may temporarily affect hearing.

# Misconceptions About Deafness and Deaf People

For many years, Deaf people were thought to be inferior to those with hearing. The phrase "deaf and dumb" had far greater implications than merely the inability to hear and speak. Deaf people were considered freaks or misfits.

Those not familiar with the past treatment of the Deaf are likely to be appalled by stories of women cloistered in religious institutions in order to hide them from view. To this day, Deaf people who have never received any education and have no language skills are being discovered by social workers and deaf advocates.

Deaf people were sent to mental institutions and homes for mentally retarded people. Some are still in those types of institutions. Boarding schools for the Deaf were thought to be dangerous places because they created opportunities for Deaf people to meet, socialize, and perhaps even (gasp!) fall in love. If Deaf people fell in love, conventional wisdom (or lack of wisdom) said Deaf people would want to marry. If they married, they would be likely to produce children, who might also be deaf.

### Sign of the Times

Jim Schneck tells of a deaf and blind woman named Nellie who was institutionalized in a state hospital for the mentally ill for 19 years. Completely cut off from language during this time, she was discovered by a Deaf volunteer who communicated with her by finger spelling into her hands. Nellie, who was institutionalized by relatives after her parents died, eventually was released from the mental hospital and attended college.

# Talk About Being Paranoid!

Members of a bizarre movement in the late part of the 1800s, led by inventor Alexander Graham Bell, claimed that the population of congenitally Deaf people in the United States was increasing at a rate higher than that of hearing people. This growing number of Deaf people posed a threat to the general population, according to Bell and his cronies, and the growth should be controlled, they said.

Deaf people were discouraged from marrying one another, or from even marrying at all. Despite that fact that Bell's own wife was deaf and his mother had severe hearing problems throughout her life, he supported eugenics, which is the science of controlling hereditary characteristics through controlled mating. Bell said loudly and often that two deaf people should not marry because it would eventually create a race of deaf people. At one point he sought to make these marriages illegal, but gave up his quest when he decided such legislation was unrealistic.

### Sign of the Times

Alexander Graham Bell's strong opinions about deaf people made him extremely controversial. Many Deaf people hated him, accusing him of attacking their identity and trying to eradicate their culture. Some Deaf people refuse to have Bell's name mentioned in their presence. Bell, however, had a great impact on education for deaf people. He contributed significant funds to educational efforts, even though those efforts were on his own terms. He financed the American Association to Promote the Teaching of Speech to the Deaf, an organization known today as Alexander Graham Bell Foundation for the Deaf.

Bell was not alone in his beliefs and efforts to control the reproduction capacities of Deaf people. It is thought that in Germany during the terrible decades of the 1930s and 1940s, about 17,000 Deaf people were surgically sterilized. If a woman happened to be pregnant when the sterilization was imposed, her baby was aborted. Another estimated 1,600 Deaf people were killed in concentration camps because they were thought to be defective and unworthy of living.

## Oppression of Deaf People

Deaf people traditionally have been subjected to the wishes of hearing people in many of the most important areas affecting their lives. Employment, social standing, their method of communication, and even their sense of identity has been affected by standards imposed by those who hear.

People who are deaf have long experienced discrimination in the workplace, and that's assuming they are able to get into a workplace at all. It is understood that certain jobs, mostly those relating to deafness and other Deaf people, are considered appropriate for people who do not hear.

So, Deaf people tend to be employed in certain areas, and under-represented, or not represented at all, in other fields. They do not, as a body, become an integrated part of society because they are not included in many areas of society. Grouping Deaf people together in certain types of jobs and professions assures that their socializing and social-ization will remain mostly with other Deaf people.

An issue that affects Deaf people much earlier in their lives than employment, however, is their struggle for identity during childhood and into adolescence.

Consider what it must be like for a Deaf child who is raised in a hearing household, as most Deaf children are. The other members of his family try desperately to make the Deaf child be like them. They want him to know their language and their culture because he is one of their family. These good intentions, however, only serve to isolate a Deaf child by ignoring or down-playing his deafness. Problems become even worse when parents refuse to learn sign language and force the child to try to speak. This severely limits the ability for communication and often serves to alienate the child.

A child who is born deaf is born into a Deaf heritage. When other family members ignore that heritage, they tell the child that his deafness is not to be recognized. It implies that his deafness is bad and that he will be more valuable if he forces himself to be like the rest of his family. On the other hand, a Deaf child raised by Deaf parents who participate in Deaf culture is immersed in that culture from birth and grows up with his own identity and heritage.

A Deaf child raised in a hearing family is often forced to turn his back on his deafness and his heritage. The situation very often changes, however, when he enters school with other Deaf people and begins to understand his identity and heritage. He is very likely to experience a sense of alienation from his family and gravitate toward other Deaf people, with whom he shares a language, a culture, and a heritage.

**Signposts**
Nine out of every 10 Deaf people marry another deaf person. It is estimated, however, that only five to 10 percent of Deaf children have Deaf parents. So much for Alexander Graham Bell's theory that two Deaf people should not have children because they are sure to be deaf, too!

**Sign of the Times**
A woman, deaf since she was about four, relates that she once traveled to France with a hearing friend. Her friend, who had studied French for five years while in school, was nonetheless unable to communicate with people in the hotels, shops, and restaurants. The Deaf woman, however, who had no experience with the language, was able to make herself understood and to understand what the French people were telling her. Her friend couldn't understand how this could be, but the Deaf woman wasn't surprised at her ability to communicate. "Why?" she says. "Because being deaf is like being in a foreign country all the time."

# Early Efforts at Educating Deaf People

Education for Deaf people has undergone some strange twists and turns during the past three and a half centuries or so. No aspect of this education, however, has been more bitterly disputed than the question of the best means of communication for Deaf people.

It was recognized and acknowledged early on that Deaf people are educable. Way back in the 1500s, a doctor in northern Italy announced that the Deaf could learn to understand written symbols by associating them with the objects they represented.

This revelation was followed by a published book of oral teaching methods for Deaf people. Juan Pablo Bonet, a Spaniard, published the book somewhere around 1620 (there are conflicting reports of the exact year). The methods were not Bonet's own, but those he had viewed while watching a teacher working with a Deaf boy. Bonet's book was called *Simplification of the Alphabet and the Art of Teaching Mutes to Speak* (so much for catchy titles!). It proved to be valuable because it raised the interest of a great many European teachers who began considering the possibility of oral education for Deaf children.

## The Great Debate Begins

Even more influential than Bonet was Charles Michel de l'Epée, a French priest who started the first school for Deaf children. Again, opinion varies on the exact year this school was started, but it's thought to be sometime in the late 1750s or the 1760s. As de l'Epée worked with the students in his school, he recognized that they communicated with each other quite well through hand signals. The priest was intrigued by this communication, and began collecting the signs, to which he added some of his own.

Although de l'Epée thought that oral communication was useful and even taught it to some of his students, he found that signing was more practical when teaching his large classes. He reasoned that teaching many Deaf children a language—even if it was a silent language—was better than teaching spoken language to only a few students.

Those who disagreed criticized de l'Epée, saying that this signed language would isolate Deaf people. The priest, who later became known as the founder of the manual approach, argued that his students should have their own identity, which they achieved through their own language. And, thus started the great debate over the value of signed language versus the value of spoken language, which still rages today.

### Sign of the Times

The story goes that de l'Epée met two young Deaf women when he stopped at their family's house to seek shelter for the night. He was moved by these women with whom he could not communicate, and concerned for the salvation of their souls. Wanting to teach them the ways of the Catholic Church, de l'Epée devised a method by which he eventually taught the women to read and write. It is said that the priest realized when meeting these women that teaching the Deaf would be his life's quest.

## The Great Debate Continues

While de l'Epée was teaching the manual approach in France, a German teacher was pushing the oral approach to Deaf education in his home country.

Samuel Heinicke, who founded the first state-supported public school for Deaf students in the late 1770s, believed that speech was necessary not only for communication, but for the development of abstract thought. He also believed that Deaf people shared with hearing people an innate desire to speak, and their desire to speak would make it easy for them to learn.

While he permitted the use of an occasional sign when explaining a complex thought, Heinicke required his students to speak aloud to each other during class and at other times when he was present.

### Sign of the Times

Heinicke's requirement of using only speech in the presence of teachers was the start of a tradition that still exists in some places. Some Deaf people say they will always associate their language—ASL—with the smell of urine. Why? Because the only place they could use ASL while in school was in the bathrooms.

Heinicke is notable in that he taught Deaf children to speak the same way hearing children learn naturally—that is, words first. Previously, it was believed that Deaf children had to learn letters before they would be able to speak words.

Heinicke and his contemporary de l'Epée had an ongoing debate concerning the best teaching methods for Deaf students. The manual approach was picking up momentum when Heinicke died in 1790, but his oral approach came back into favor many years later when hearing educators decided—with no input from Deaf people—that it was better for the Deaf to speak and speech read than to sign.

> **Sign of the Times**
>
> Talk about being way off base! In Heinicke's day, it was widely believed that a Deaf person's inability to speak was caused by a defect of the tongue, not a lack of hearing. Many children were subjected to operations attempting to correct nonexistent problems with their tongues. Heinicke, by the way, recognized that the inability to speak was a result of deafness and opposed this practice.

# From France and Germany to the U.S.A.

A few decades later in New England, a Connecticut theologian named Thomas Hopkins Gallaudet opened the United States' first permanent school for Deaf students.

Gallaudet, a brilliant scholar who entered Yale University at age 14 and graduated first in his class at age 17, became intrigued with teaching Deaf students when he happened to meet Alice Cogswell, the nine-year-old daughter of a Hartford doctor. Gallaudet, who by this time had earned a divinity degree from Andover Theological Seminary and was planning to be a minister, met Cogswell in 1814, when he was 27.

He was successful with teaching the young girl the manual alphabet and some reading skills, and Gallaudet was persuaded (in part by the girl's father) to go to Europe to learn more about teaching Deaf students.

He studied in Paris with Abbé Roch Ambroise Cucurron Sicard, head of the Institut Royal des Sourds-Muets (now the Institute National de Jeunes Sourds). While there, he met teacher Laurent Clerc, a young Frenchman who had been deaf since he was a year old and had also studied under Sicard.

With Sicard's blessing, Clerc returned to the United States with Gallaudet, and together they opened the Asylum for the Education and Instruction of the Deaf and Dumb (now called the American School for the Deaf) in Hartford in 1817.

## Sign of the Times

When Laurent Clerc returned to America with Thomas Hopkins Gallaudet, he planned to stay for three years and then return to France. His plans, however, changed when he became a teacher at Gallaudet's school for Deaf students in Hartford. He fell in love with Eliza Boardman, one of the school's original students. They were married in 1818, just one year after the school opened. Clerc decided to stay in America, and he taught for 50 years before retiring at the age of 73. He died in 1869 and is buried in Hartford, next to Eliza.

Clerc and Gallaudet used the manual method of education, establishing a standardized version that combined existing signs with new signs and employed some of the rules of French sign language. The school became extremely popular not only with students from New England, but from other parts of the country as well. The school received financial aid from the U.S. government and continued to expand. By the mid-1800s, there were schools for Deaf students in 12 states and the first college for Deaf students had opened in Washington, D.C. and was run by Gallaudet's son, Edward Miner Gallaudet.

The college, first called the Columbia Institution for the Deaf, is the present-day esteemed Gallaudet University. It was officially chartered in 1864.

# Doing What Comes Naturally

Sign language flourished in Hartford and in other schools for Deaf students across the country. It is thought that Clerc adapted his French Sign Language to English, and taught the revised language to the teachers and students in Gallaudet's school. Clerc's reputation as an excellent teacher spread, and soon teachers from different states were coming to Connecticut to learn his sign language.

Clerc's language, combined with the home signs that students at Hartford and various other schools brought with them and shared with one another, new signs that were generated as it became necessary, and some pantomime, formed the basis for American Sign Language.

A common language grew out of the various signed languages and dialects that students brought to their schools. Called a contact language, the new sign language was passed on to the next generation. The quality of education for Deaf students in America, who used sign language easily and happily, had exceeded expectations.

## Uh-Oh, Here Comes Trouble

Not content to leave well enough alone, some prominent American educators of the mid-1800s decided that sign language used by itself was inappropriate.

Samuel Gridley Howe and Horace Mann returned from a visit to Europe just raving about the German schools for Deaf students. These schools, they reported, used only spoken German. German Deaf students, they said, know how to speak, while American students do not.

In the late 1860s, Howe was behind the formation of a school for Deaf students in Massachusetts. The school (now known as the Clarke School) required that spoken English be used at all times. A similar school opened soon after in New York. It was about this time that Alexander Graham Bell got involved with education for Deaf people and came out strongly in support of the oralist movement.

## From Bad to Worse

Edward Miner Gallaudet was Bell's primary opponent. Gallaudet advocated the dual use of sign language and written English, with some spoken English also to be used if possible for a student to do so. But Gallaudet was in the minority, and the use of sign language was discontinued in nearly all American and European schools for Deaf students.

**Warning Sign**
The debate over signed versus spoken language is not restricted to educators and administrators. Deaf people have their own share of disagreement about the matter. A man named Mike, who is profoundly deaf since birth, expressed his opinion: "I can speak and lip-read well, and I do not know sign language at all," Mike wrote. "To survive in the everyday world, a Deaf or Hard-of-Hearing person must know how to lip-read and speak."

By the early 1900s, sign language was not only out of vogue, it was strictly forbidden in many schools. There were many more schools for Deaf students than there had been 50 years before, but they were almost entirely oral schools. It appeared that sign language would continue to be suppressed and eventually forgotten.

## The Comeback of ASL

Educators who favored the oral approach, however, underestimated the tenacity and power of students who understood that sign was their natural language.

Students, under risk of penalty, continued to use ASL in their dormitories, on the playing fields, and in other social situations. Deaf parents of Deaf children continued to use the language at home and taught it to their children. It remained a suppressed but by no means forgotten language.

The great debate continues to this day. If signed language is better than spoken language for Deaf people, then what form of signed language should be used? Is signed language really better than spoken language?

ASL, although certainly not accepted by everyone, is gaining ground. There is great interest in the language, reflected by the increase of ASL classes, instructional videos, and books. It has been incorporated with other methods of communication, such as Signed English, speech reading, and speech in many educational programs for deaf students of all ages.

# The Least You Need to Know

> ➤ Causes of deafness can range from prenatal problems, childhood diseases, and inherited deafness to adult or drug-induced hearing loss.

> ➤ There always have been, and still are, many misconceptions concerning deafness and Deaf people.

> ➤ There has been strong disagreement for centuries over the best methods of communication for Deaf people.

> ➤ Some of the great advocates for Deaf people are Charles Michel de l'Epée, Juan Pablo Bonet, Laurent Clerc, and Thomas Hopkins Gallaudet.

> ➤ ASL, once banned from nearly every school for Deaf students, is making a comeback.

> ➤ Gallauden University (Washington, D.C.)

> ➤ The American School for the Deaf (Hartford, Connecticut)

> ➤ The Clarke School (Northampton, Massachusetts)

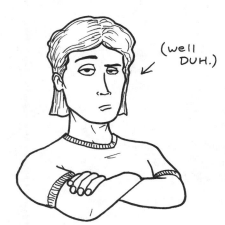

(well DUH.)

# But, Is It Really a Language?

This is something we can clear up quickly. The answer to the question presented in the title is a resounding *yes*. ASL is a language.

For a long time, it was generally agreed upon that a language had to be spoken. After all, the word itself implies speech. *Language* comes from the Latin word *lingua*, for which the literal translation is *tongue*.

So, what is this method of communication—ASL—that is neither spoken nor heard, but seen? Research conducted within the past few decades has shown that ASL is a complete language that Deaf people acquire naturally, just as hearing people acquire a spoken language. We'll look later in this chapter at how Deaf children learn ASL in much the same way hearing children learn the languages used in their homes.

Just for fun, though, we'll explore some of the arguments and look at why those who are not in the know still try to discredit ASL as a legitimate language.

# What's In a Word?

William Stokoe, a scholar of linguistics who extensively studied ASL, pronounced in 1960 that it was, indeed, a language. He showed that signing is as linguistically complex as speech, and draws on many of the same parts of the brain that speaking does.

Stokoe's work was the first serious study of this language, and gradually paved the way for more general acceptance of ASL. When Stokoe, who was a faculty member at Gallaudet University, first released his findings, however, they met with resistance from both Deaf and hearing people. His own colleagues scoffed at his paper, "Sign Language Structure," and those in the field of special education tried to discredit it completely.

More surprising than the attacks from the academic community, however, were those from the Deaf community. Rather than being hailed for his serious consideration of their language, Stokoe was denounced by some Deaf people who resented his analysis of ASL. One theory for this behavior is that native users of ASL feared that such scientific analysis might result in changes to their language, of which they were extremely protective.

Since Stokoe's original findings were released, more and more people, both deaf and hearing, have publicly and privately agreed with them.

More recently, Stokoe and two other experts, David Armstrong and Sherman Wilcox, have conducted further studies and written a new book called *Gesture and Nature of Language*. In this book, they argue that signing is not only a complete and legitimate language, but may have been the very first language. Our early ancestors very likely used a form of sign language to communicate, the scholars assert. Sign language eventually gave way to spoken language, but vestiges of sign language remain.

**A Good Sign**
Some scholars feel that all people have an innate sense of sign language, but that assertion could even extend beyond humans to animals. Some chimpanzees and gorillas also seem to have an aptitude toward sign language, easily learning and using ASL signs and stringing signs together to convey thoughts.

Armstrong, an anthropologist, asserts that all people have an innate sense of sign language. "People who have no contact with Deaf people use a whole repertoire of manual gestures, and some are identical to the signs in sign language," he says. "We all have some common stock of signs."

ASL is a visual language, but not a pictorial one. A pictorial language, such as pantomime, does not employ grammar. ASL, on the other hand, has its own grammar that dictates the way words and sentences are formed. It can communicate not only concrete objects, as a pictorial language would be limited to, but thoughts, feelings, and many other abstracts, as well.

Even though ASL has been recognized as a true language, many people still disagree. The thought that words must have sounds and that a language is heard and not seen is still prevalent. Sign language is still considered by many to be a crude or primitive form of language. Stokoe, Armstrong, and Wilcox hope their book will serve to enlighten. "One of the motivations of my work is to let people know that Deaf people are just as bright and able to handle abstract thought as hearing people, given equal education," Stokoe says. "Prejudice against them because they don't speak leads to all sorts of bad judgments about Deaf people. The fact that we all probably owe a great deal to the era when language began in a gestural state might change some of that."

# What's So Special About ASL?

Given the opportunity to learn ASL as their native language, Deaf children will learn in a manner very similar to that of how hearing children learn to speak. They babble—only with their hands—just as a hearing child would with sounds. Hearing children next progress to a one-word stage, where the Deaf child makes one sign at a time. They make mistakes when forming signs, just as hearing children do as they mispronounce words.

Some researchers feel that Deaf children learn ASL faster and earlier than hearing children learn their spoken language, but opinion on that varies. Some parents of children who begin learning sign language at birth, though, say there is no question that signing comes well before speaking. A father says his three children all started signing at somewhere between six and eight months. At that point, he says, they were able to communicate their needs with signs such as *milk*, *wet*, and *afraid*. A Deaf mother said all three of her kids signed before they spoke. The first signs for two of her children were *cookie*, while her other son's first sign was *more*.

Studies do show that a child learning to sign generally has more signs in his vocabulary at a young age than hearing children have words. A child learning to sign will progress to two words, then add pronouns, word order, and other aspects of language at about the same age and in the same order as a hearing child learning to speak.

### Sign of the Times

Some studies suggest that motor control of the hands occurs earlier than control of the vocal apparatus, making sign language easier to catch on to at a very young age than spoken language. Experts are not sure about this, and some say that Deaf children may learn to sign earlier than hearing children learn to speak because the tools for communicating (the hands) are visible and can be fashioned and molded into the proper positions.

These parallels between how signed and spoken language are learned have led some scientists to believe that the brain has a natural tendency to learn language in a certain progression—regardless of the form of language.

# When Learning the Language is Delayed

The playing field becomes unlevel as far as ASL is concerned, however, because of the many variables found in the early lives of Deaf people. Of course, there are also variables among hearing people, but hearing children who for some reason are not exposed to language in their homes, most likely will be exposed to it elsewhere at a very early age. Deaf children who are not exposed to signing in their homes, however, may have no exposure to any language for years.

Many Deaf children are not diagnosed until they are more than a year old. By that time, they have already fallen behind in exposure to language. If nobody in the child's home uses sign language, there is no model for language. The child must come up with his own means of communication, such as pushing his sister out of the way when he wants to get by her, or grabbing his toy away from the cousin who has borrowed it. He gets his point across, but not in a way the other people in his home consider acceptable.

**Signposts**

Julia, who has been Deaf since she was four, remembers repeatedly taking off the hearing aids her mother insisted she wear when she was a little girl. She hated the hearing aids more than anything else, Julia says, but understands now that her mother thought she was doing what was best for her when she had Julia fitted for them. Julia says she resented her mother for a long time for not accepting her the way she was, but trying to make her daughter like herself—hearing.

When the child is reprimanded for these actions, he is being denied the chance to communicate at all and becomes increasingly frustrated. The child knows that something is wrong, but doesn't know what or how to fix it. The parents are also frustrated by their inability to communicate effectively with their child, and a series of negative exchanges occur.

Sociologists say it is natural for parents to want to pass along their own values, beliefs, and heritage to their children. Hence, hearing parents of a Deaf child often have a natural reaction to try to make their child like they are, despite the child's deafness.

It is surprising how many parents of Deaf children never learn to sign, but insist that their children communicate on their terms. This sometimes causes permanent damage in the parent/child relationship. Ideally, hearing parents and Deaf children, or Deaf parents and hearing children, will accommodate each other's needs and learn any possible means of communicating.

# Professional Advice Can Help—or Hurt

Parents may consult numerous professionals in different areas. Audiologists, health care professionals, counselors, and psychologists might get involved in the diagnosis and treatment of the Deaf child. Parents may get conflicting advice from these professionals and become confused about what's best for their child.

Staff members at the university were encouraged at Peter's chances to learn speech. Instead of buying into the total communication plan, though, they instructed Jim and his wife to immediately cease using ASL in Peter's presence and to force the boy to speak to them.

Jim was furious at their proposal, feeling that it denied ASL and everything Deaf people had worked for. Although Peter learned some speech, ASL remained his language and has served him well. "My son is 21 now and still doesn't have good speech," Jim says. "But he has excellent language skills."

Jim says this story is an example of the kind of pressure that parents of Deaf children receive all the time. Parents who are not well informed about ASL and Deaf issues often rely on whatever advice professionals give them, instead of studying all the options and deciding what would be best for their child.

It is not unusual for parents to deny their child's deafness and try to make the child act like he is hearing. They might force him to learn to speak, even though it is a tremendous undertaking. They might insist that hearing aids be used, whether or not they do much good. In some cases, cochlea implants are given to Deaf children in hopes of making them able to hear. The implants, which are surgically implanted in the mastoid bone to stimulate the hearing nerve, do not allow the person to hear normally, but have resulted in improved hearing in some cases. Many Deaf people vehemently oppose these implants, particularly when they are imposed on children. They feel that to try to make a Deaf person hear by use of such drastic measures, negates the sum of who the person is. Many Deaf people view their deafness as a condition, but not an impairment. It is a characteristic similar to height or hair color.

**Warning Sign**
When Kim was diagnosed as having a severe hearing loss when she was a freshman in high school, her mother refused to acknowledge the situation. As a result, Kim was left to continue her lonely struggle to effectively communicate. "It was one of those situations where I fell through the cracks," she says. "I did not get the information and/ or counseling that I should have. I didn't know about devices like flashing alarms and stuff that could have helped me cope better." Kim eventually did learn about such devices, learned ASL, and came to understand Deaf culture. It was not, however, an easy journey.

It is ironic that hearing parents rarely seek out the advice of Deaf adults or older Deaf children when trying to figure out the best course to take for their Deaf child. Professionals have been faulted by members of the Deaf community for not advising parents to do this.

Obviously, Deaf children born into homes where ASL is used have a great language advantage over Deaf children in homes where it is not used. Signing is learned naturally and from birth, giving way to communication in the early months of a child's life. Some people still argue that Deaf people are better served being taught to speak and lip-read so that they can function in the hearing world. This assertion is hotly contested by many, many Deaf people, who call ASL their language and the language of their culture.

# Signals in the Air

A non-signing, hearing person watching two people conversing in ASL might well be intimidated or feel left out. Imagine what it would be like: hands moving rapidly through the air, accompanied by a spectrum of facial expressions, all of which obviously mean something significant to the people involved in the conversation. As a hearing person, however, you would have no idea what was being communicated. You may resent the signers because you can't understand them. Or, the sight might inspire feelings of admiration and respect for those who have mastered this language.

**Signposts**
A Deaf woman, Kathy, often expresses feelings of isolation and the difficulty of trying to communicate with people who don't use ASL. Most hearing people, she says, will never understand the frustrations that go along with an inability to communicate. Her own husband, though, who is hearing, got a taste of what it is like when he accompanied her on a visit to Gallaudet University. "There I was a native and he was the 'outsider,'" Kathy said. "It really opened his eyes to how I feel and struggle every day to communicate."

A witness of the Gallaudet Revolution in 1988 (we'll learn more about the Revolution later in this chapter) Oliver Sacks, the hearing author of *Seeing Voices: A Journey Into the World of the Deaf*, recalls how he felt as he watched Deaf students using their language during the Gallaudet event. As this hearing person watched the Revolution, he was stricken by the intensity and beauty of the signing occurring all around him. Although he understood nothing of the signing going on, he sensed the passion and intensity of the signers.

Using sign language is a triumph for Deaf people. It not only provides an effective means of communication, it signals autonomy and self-reliance. Using these signals in the air tells the world that Deaf people are proud and united, not a group to be pitied or put down.

# Call Them Accents

While ASL is known as the language of the Deaf, it varies depending on where it's used and who is using it. We've already learned that there are many different sign languages in many different countries. But, within ASL, there are many variables.

The signed language of people who learned English before learning ASL is different in its use of grammar and form than that of native users of ASL.

Geographical differences also factor into these variations of ASL. People from different parts of the country will give different signs for the same words in many cases. Experts think that in the early 1800s, Deaf people from different parts of the country who used sign language would not have been able to communicate with one another. It simply would not have been possible because the signs were too different.

Once Gallaudet and Clerc's school for the Deaf got underway in 1817, however, a more centralized form of sign language occurred. Children came to the school from different parts of the country to learn sign language, and took that language home with them when they returned. Some of Gallaudet's and Clerc's students set up schools of their own and passed along this more standardized version of sign language. These signs were mixed with regional signs, which account for the differences that still exist.

### Sign of the Times

Edgar H. and Susan P. Schroyer, authors of *Signs Across America: A Look at Regional Differences in American Sign Language*, say that their surveys showed there are 16 different signs for *hot dog* among sign language users in 25 states. Twenty-two signs for *picnic* were gathered from the 25 states represented, 16 for *squirrel*, and seven for *spinach*. Some of the signs even varied within the same state!

There is also a form of ASL found in use among black Deaf people in the southern part of the U.S. This dialect was developed among black Deaf children who had their own schools before desegregation. The dialect is so different that other ASL users usually understand only part of what is being signed. And, in Hawaii, sign language does not reflect the teachings of Clerc and Gallaudet at all.

Everybody learning ASL should be aware of these variations in case you encounter them when using the language. Remember that these *accents* are common, just as they are in spoken language, and be flexible.

# It's More Than Just a Language, Man

ASL is much more than a language. It is part of the rich collection of values, history, and ideas that make up Deaf culture. It is an integral part of the identity of Deaf people. And it is a common bond between Deaf people who often feel the hearing world does not value their culture.

A noted leader of the Deaf community said, ASL is such an important part of who a Deaf person is, that to reject the language is to reject the person. She also suggested that if hearing people would widely learn to use ASL, Deaf people would lose their identity because the language would no longer belong to them.

Deaf users of ASL tend to be possessive of their language, simply because it is theirs. It is not a language forced upon them by well-meaning parents or educators who can't fully understand the difficulties of learning it. ASL is a language created by Deaf people over the years. It belongs to them.

While it unites those who are Deaf, ASL separates its users from the hearing world. And, just as Deaf people become frustrated when they can't understand a spoken conversation, hearing people who don't sign are sometimes uncomfortable in the presence of signers. And, while most Deaf people welcome the efforts of hearing people who learn ASL, hearing people must remember that learning the language of Deaf culture does not make them members of the culture. Even Jim Schneck, who is fluent in ASL, works with the Deaf community everyday, and has adopted a Deaf son, says he will never be accepted into the inner circle of Deaf culture. Why? Because he isn't Deaf.

**Signposts**

Cindy and her sister, Denise, both of whom were born Deaf and are native users of ASL, laugh as they remember visiting their hearing cousins. The cousins always regarded them with suspicion, Cindy said, because they couldn't understand them. She said the sisters would have great fun signing in front of their cousins, and always felt a bit of satisfaction when the tables were turned and they were the ones who understood, while others were left out in the cold.

# Coming Home

Deaf people who first experience ASL after struggling to learn English or being denied any language at all describe it as a feeling of coming home.

Edmund Booth, a 19th-century teacher and journalist who attended Thomas Gallaudet's American School for the Deaf in Hartford, recalled in his autobiography the feeling he had when he and his brother first encountered students using ASL: "Charles and I went into the boys' and next the girls' sitting rooms," Booth writes. "It was all new to me and to Charles (who was hearing) it was amusing, the innumerable motions of arms and hands. After dinner, he (Charles) left and I was among strangers but I knew I was home."

The desire to be with people who speak the same language and share the same beliefs and values is natural and widespread. It is no wonder that Deaf people have their own clubs, schools, theater, and dance groups. It is no wonder that Deaf people are so nurturing and protective of their culture.

# The Revolution

Most hearing people have little knowledge or awareness of Deaf culture. It was thrust into the limelight in 1988, however, when students at Gallaudet University shut down the school in a week-long protest that has become known as the Gallaudet Revolution.

The Revolution began spontaneously on Sunday, March 6, when it was announced that Elisabeth Ann Zinser, vice chancellor for academic affairs at the University of North Carolina at Greensboro had been named president of Gallaudet. Zinser was the only hearing person of the final three candidates, and had little or no experience with Deaf people, ASL, or Deaf culture.

Students at the university had made very clear their desire for a Deaf president. Three thousand people attended a rally on campus the week before the appointment was made to express their feelings to the board of trustees, and students held a candlelight vigil the night before the appointment was announced.

A group of students and staff members who had gathered to hear the announcement were outraged when they learned Zinser had been named. The outrage intensified as word spread, and the next day more than 1,000 students marched to the hotel in which the board of trustees had gathered.

On Tuesday, students barricaded all entrances to the campus and the university was forced to close. By Wednesday, the faculty and staff had come out in support of the students and the four demands they had expressed:

➤ A Deaf president be appointed immediately.

➤ Jane Bassett Spilman, chairwoman of the board of trustees (who had been reported to say that Deaf people were not yet ready to function in the hearing world), would resign immediately.

➤ The board of trustees be required to have a 51 percent majority of Deaf members (at that time only four of the 21 members were Deaf).

➤ There would be no reprisals against those involved in the Revolution.

National media coverage drew more attention to the situation, and support for the students swelled. A communications center with teams of interpreters for reporters was set up. Greg Hlibok, one of the students who led the protest, appeared on ABC's *Nightline* show with Deaf actress Marlee Matlin.

On Friday, March 11, supporters from all over America joined Gallaudet students for a march to the U.S. Capitol. More than 3,000 strong, the marchers were cheered along the way and praised during the rally at the Capitol.

On Sunday, a week after the original announcement, Dr. I. King Jordan, dean of the Gallaudet's College of Arts and Sciences, was named the university's first Deaf president. Spilman resigned from the board of trustees, and it was pledged that the board would be adapted to give it a majority of Deaf members. Board members pledged there would be no reprisals against students.

Changes continued at Gallaudet following the Revolution. More emphasis was placed on ASL, and more Deaf people were added to the faculty and staff. A new major in Deaf Studies was instituted.

The Gallaudet Revolution was a turning point for Deaf people and Deaf culture. It gave power to Deaf students and their supporters, and let the world know they were forces with which to be reckoned.

### Sign of the Times

If you'd like more information and insights about the Gallaudet Revolution, try these books:

➤ *The Week the World Heard Gallaudet* by J. Gannon (Gallaudet University Press, 1989)

➤ *Deaf President Now! The 1988 Revolution at Gallaudet University* by J.B. Christiansen and S.N. Barnartt (Gallaudet University Press, 1995)

The following year, an event called The Deaf Way was held in Washington, D.C., to celebrate the culture of Deaf people. Artists, political representatives, scholars, and many others gathered to declare their pride and commitment to Deaf culture.

Understanding that Deaf culture is the essence of a Deaf person's identity, and that ASL is intricately entwined with Deaf culture, it's easy to see why the language is more than a language to those who use it.

# The Least You Need to Know

➤ ASL has been scientifically proven to be a complete language, even though it is not a spoken language.

➤ There are many similarities in the way that babies learn to speak and to sign.

➤ There are various factors that determine if, and when, a Deaf child will learn ASL. These include whether or not the parents are Deaf, where the child is sent to school, and what sort of advice parents are given concerning the child's education.

➤ ASL is a language of grace and passion that inspires great emotion from those who use it and those who watch it being used.

➤ If you live in Michigan and use ASL, expect to notice some differences in the signs when you travel to South Carolina. There are many regional differences in signs.

➤ The 1988 Gallaudet Revolution brought attention to Deaf culture and raised public awareness of issues concerning the Deaf.

➤ ASL is an integral part of Deaf culture and a source of identity among the people who use it.

(I am VERY frustrated)

# Chapter 4

# I'll Never Get This—Will I?

## In This Chapter

➤ Realizing that learning to sign is a commitment

➤ Using the dictionary

➤ Understanding the limits of illustrations

➤ Watching your progress can certainly help

➤ Looking for creative ways to practice ASL

By now you should have a better understanding of the origins and history of ASL and how Deaf people have struggled to have it recognized as a legitimate and *real* language. Hopefully, you've also gotten some idea of the obstacles and challenges that Deaf people face every day, and an appreciation for the richness of Deaf culture.

It should be understood, though, that we've barely scratched the surface on these complex topics. We encourage you to look for some of the many books available on deafness and Deaf culture, and to do some further reading.

In this chapter we'll start to explore the learning process for ASL. We'll explain how the sign dictionary should be used and give you some tips to make learning ASL easier. We'll also discuss the limitations of learning ASL from a book.

# What Will It Take?

There are many possible reasons why you decided you want to learn to sign. Maybe you know a Deaf person and want to be able to communicate. Or, perhaps you think it will enhance your employability or help you in your job. Maybe you're just intrigued by the grace, energy, and beauty of the language and want to share in it.

Whatever your reasons are for wanting to learn to sign, it is important to remember something. This book will give you reliable and sound information about ASL and related topics, and teach you many signs you'll need to know when using ASL. It will give you an excellent start on your journey into sign language, and the ability to communicate in sign to a certain extent. You will not, however, be an expert in sign language when you finish the last chapter of this book.

Those of you who have studied a foreign language like Spanish or German probably can remember the frustration you felt during the process. You learned all you could from the books, teacher or tapes. You felt like you were making good progress as you completed grammar drills and recited sentences. And then, you tried to use the language with somebody who really knew it and fell flat on your face. Sound familiar? It will be the same way with ASL. And, just as with Spanish or German, if you keep practicing and working, you'll eventually wonder why you thought it was so hard.

Just like with any language, learning ASL will be work. It will take commitment, motivation, and practice.

Although basic communication skills can be learned in just a few months, it generally takes between five and seven years from the time learning starts for a person to be fluent in sign language. This is the general timetable for attaining fluency in spoken languages, as well. The learning process is accelerated, of course, if the student spends a lot of time communicating with native signers. Someone hoping to become a good interpreter for the Deaf should count on a couple more years of learning time, preferably spent in a formal training program.

Deaf people are extremely (and understandably) irritated by people who learn a little ASL and claim to be very knowledgeable or even an *expert* on the subject. It's a little like somebody who has completed a first-aid course trying to pass himself off as a physician.

A Deaf woman consulted during the writing of this book expressed her frustration and annoyance by these instant experts. "Why is it that hearing people think they take one or two sign language classes and they are qualified to be interpreters?" wrote Kim Horn, who is Deaf and has taught sign language for many years. "Do you take two courses of French and become an interpreter? Of course not! A person may like sign language and like to sign, but that doesn't make them an interpreter. It is akin to me saying I am a singer. Sure, I like music. I like to sing. But that does not mean I am a singer."

So read, work, and practice, and you'll have some good, basic ASL skills when you're finished with this book. Don't, however, insult Deaf people and Deaf culture by claiming to be a seasoned signer.

Do ask someone who uses ASL as his or her first language for help if you're lucky enough to know such a person. Watch closely at how the person forms signs, uses finger spelling, and puts everything together.

### Sign of the Times

It is very difficult for hearing people to understand how protective Deaf people feel toward ASL—their language. Although most Deaf people are willing to help a hearing person learn ASL, many feel that hearing people can not effectively teach or write about the language or Deaf culture. The reason for this, according to one Deaf man, is that the language is the only thing that has really belonged exclusively to Deaf people.

# Using the Dictionary

The dictionary section of this book is grouped in natural categories instead of listed alphabetically. For instance, if you want the sign for *horse*, *tiger*, *frog*, or *flower*, you'd turn to Chapter 13, "Pets and Other Beasts."

Some categories, however, might not be quite so clear. If you're trying to figure out how to sign *please*, *thank you*, or *Was that really your foot, I'm so sorry*, you might not know that they are contained in Chapter 16, called "Celebrations and Occasions."

Don't despair or start tearing out pages, though. Simply use the index in the back of the book to find what you need. All the words contained within the dictionary are listed there.

Understandably, you're anxious to get to the dictionary and start signing. Before you do that, though, you're going to need to do some work in advance. There are some things you've got to know about before you start signing. Handshape, the finger spelled alphabet, and numbers will be very important as you begin learning signs. In fact, you can't learn signs without understanding handshapes, because your hands must be shaped in a particular way in order to make a sign.

You'll also need to know where to hold your hands in relation to your body when signing, palm position, and some other important aspects of sign language. We'll cover these topics more thoroughly in the next section of the book.

So, you'll have to study and then practice handshapes, numbers, and the manual alphabet. After that you'll plow your way through the dictionary. Guess what? There will still be more to learn before you'll really begin to feel comfortable using sign language.

## Siglish

The tendency for English-speaking people who are learning sign language is to choose the corresponding signs for what they want to say in English, and then string the signs together into an English-style sentence.

**Warning Sign**
Deaf people almost never use simultaneous conversation amongst themselves. Many Deaf people were forced to use speech in their schools and even at home, and feel that it is a denial of their own language and culture.

**Signposts**
A former public school teacher who worked with Deaf students says she observed sim-com on a daily basis while teaching. "The idea was to speak and sign simultaneously," she said. "Of course, what really resulted was the teachers would talk and throw in a few signs. Frankly, I am amazed that the kids understood any of it. ASL is not a visual representation of English. You can't speak English and sign at the same time."

Well, you can do that, and somebody who is fluent in sign will probably be able to get a general idea of what you're trying to say. But that method, called Pidgin Sign English, or *Siglish*, is awkward and not true signing. Most fluent signers will be patient with those using Pidgin Sign English if they understand it is only the first step in learning sign language. But to learn sign language only to the Pidgin stage is not doing justice to a beautiful, expressive language.

## Sim-Com

Another method of communication between a Deaf and hearing person—especially a hearing person who is learning, but not yet proficient in sign language—is simultaneous communication. Simultaneous communication, or "sim-com," is also commonly used when there is a group of people that includes someone who can't sign.

Sim-com combines the use of speech, signs, and finger spelling, and is valued because it offers the benefit of seeing two forms of a message at the same time. A Deaf person speech-reads what is being spoken, while reading the signs and finger spelling of the speaker at the same time. Sim-com is used in many Deaf schools across the country, but can be controversial because it fits into neither the oral nor manual approach.

While considered useful for learning signers, sim-com presents some problems. It is difficult to speak and sign at the same time, and conversation relayed by this method is generally slow and cumbersome. If a hearing person tries to speed up the process by eliminating some of the signs that are accompanying his speech, the Deaf person may have trouble following.

So, if you're tempted to try sim-com, keep in mind that it's imperfect and may actually make communication more difficult.

# Not by Book Alone

Although this book is organized and geared toward teaching readers a lot of signs in various categories, there are some limitations that come with any illustrated book of sign language.

As skilled as our artists are, it is very difficult to indicate hand movements with illustrations. We use arrows to show you in what directions hands should move, and some written instructions as well. Hopefully, this combination of instructions will do the trick. We realize, however, and you should too, that there is a possibility for error if the instructions are misinterpreted or not followed properly.

Also, there is not a corresponding sign for every word in the English language. A signer must know how to choose a sign that expresses her thought, even though there may not be a sign for the exact word she has in mind. Experts say the manner in which a signer uses sign language is more important than the number of signs she knows. Remember, there are a lot of subtleties, such as facial expression and hand position, that go along with signing.

Of course, we're not trying to play down the importance of learning enough signs to communicate your thoughts. Obviously, if you're trying to tell your buddy that the football game starts at 3 p.m., it won't do to substitute the sign for *party* for the sign for *football*. Your buddy will no doubt be confused when he learns there is no party, and probably will be inappropriately dressed for a football game.

Again, the best way of learning any language is to associate with people who use that language. While we cover many signs, no book can do justice to the slang, idioms, and other nuances that are an important part of American Sign Language.

# Helping Yourself

A mirror can be very useful when learning sign language, and especially in the early stages when you're learning finger spelling. Practicing finger spelling in front of a mirror will reinforce your knowledge of how to make the shapes.

Try teaching finger spelling to a friend or family member, and have them finger spell to you so you get some practice reading as well as signing.

It is important to keep your hands steady while finger spelling. Experts say the tendency for many beginners is to jerk their hands up and down while finger spelling. Keep your hands in the same place and try to keep an even rhythm.

It takes some time and practice to get your fingers moving quickly when finger spelling. It's quite easy to learn the shapes, but trickier to make your fingers do what you want them to as quickly as you'd like. Just like anything else, the more you practice, the faster you'll become adept. Remember how awkward it was when you first started typing or playing the piano or guitar? You'll feel the same way when you start signing. Just as with the piano, signing will soon come naturally.

Remember, though, experts stress that accuracy is far more important in finger spelling than speed. If the person you're signing to doesn't understand you, it doesn't matter how fast you are!

Kim, the ASL teacher we met earlier in this chapter, tells her students to practice finger spelling while they drive. Caution please! Practicing while driving is one thing. Practicing while driving, drinking a cup of coffee, and talking on your cell phone is something quite different—and *not* recommended! The teacher says she sees quick improvement in those students who finger spell street names, the make of the car in front of them, and so on. Finger spelling newspaper headlines is another good way to practice.

**Signposts**

When you first start practicing signs, you'll probably feel very awkward and unsure. Your movements will seem stilted and sometimes not very natural. Don't be discouraged! This is completely normal. Just hang in there and keep practicing.

A video camera can also help you to check your progress. Set up your camera and tape yourself, or you exhibitionists can get somebody to record you. Make yourself a list of some sentences to sign and go ahead. You might be surprised at what you see.

Remember that sign language involves more than your hands. The first few times you have the opportunity to watch fluent signers in action, you are likely to be surprised by how much facial expression and body language is used. While the hands move in front of the body, the body is by no means stationary. Signers will lean toward the person to whom they're speaking, then back away for another sign.

**A Good Sign**

"Most of my beginning sign language students are commuters to (Washington) D.C. and spend a lot of time in their cars," Kimberly Horn says. "Signing to music gives them great practice and is something they can do to use up time when they're sitting in traffic on the beltway."

Signing songs is great practice when learning sign language because it builds rhythm. Kim tells her students to figure out the best way to sign a song conceptually, tape it, and then watch to see if they've come up with an accurate and pleasant-to-watch translation. Watching yourself as you practice signing will make you more aware of your facial expressions and body language.

Once you decide that you're going to learn ASL, you'll need to make a commitment to practice. Most people find they get so caught up in the energy and fun of the language that practicing is a pleasure.

# Practice Makes Perfect—Well, Almost

Once you've started to get the hang of using sign language, you'll probably be anxious to practice anywhere and with anyone you can. The energy of sign language is contagious; you can't help but get caught up in it.

If you're serious about practicing sign language and becoming involved with Deaf people and Deaf culture, you'll have to go to where Deaf people are. A good place to start might be an agency in your area that provides services for Deaf people. There is a wonderful agency in Lancaster, Pennsylvania, called the Deaf and Hard-of-Hearing Services of Lancaster County.

The agency is usually filled with people conversing in sign language. They share news that particularly affects Deaf people and talk about politics, sports, and the weather. Deaf and hard of hearing people stop by for support and encouragement, or for help with a complicated phone call. They might want advice concerning a legal or medical issue, or require some counseling. They might want some help finding housing, or stop by to thank a staff member for his or her help with a previous matter. Many come by just to say hello and chat for a bit. The office is a mecca for someone who wants to observe or participate in signing.

Someone genuinely interested in learning sign language and more about Deaf culture could volunteer at an agency such as the one in Lancaster. There no doubt would be copies to be made, filing to be done, and so forth. But such an experience would provide many insights into Deaf culture and opportunities to practice sign language with real experts—those who use it as their primary language.

## Sign of the Times

As an example, Jill, a friend who learned sign language in college and now works with Deaf children, was reminiscing about an experience she had shortly after she started her first job. She was invited to a gathering at the home of a colleague, at which several Deaf people were present. She was anxious to communicate in sign language, and joined a group of Deaf people at one end of the room. To her dismay, she discovered she was nowhere near ready to sign with these people who used the language constantly. She said her hands felt like lead, and she couldn't understand half of what was being signed. Humbled, she watched the group joke and laugh in sign language. She understood then that she had a long way to go to really learn the language of the Deaf.

Other places where you could observe and perhaps participate in signed conversations are churches where sign language is used during the service, schools for Deaf children, theaters and concerts for the Deaf, and sporting events with Deaf participants.

The point is, you can learn signs from a book, but you can't learn sign language from a book. Sign language is a whole package, delivered best by the people to whom it belongs.

## The Least You Need to Know

➤ Deafness and Deaf culture are complex topics that require extensive study.

➤ A sign language course or two does not make someone an expert.

➤ A dictionary alone is not enough to teach you to sign.

➤ How you sign something, using a facial expression and body language, is as important as the signs you use.

➤ Lights, camera, action—practicing with a mirror, video camera, or radio can help you learn sign language more quickly.

➤ Be creative when looking for places to practice sign language, and don't overlook volunteering at agencies or other places where Deaf people gather.

# Part 2
# Preparing to Learn ASL

At this point, everybody is ready to jump right in and start signing. But not so fast there! There are some preliminaries we need to get out of the way.

American Sign Language is a natural language, but it's got a lot of little things you need to know in order to do it correctly. For instance, you can't sign without facial expression. It would be worse than speaking in a complete monotone. It just isn't done.

Plus, you've got to learn the manual alphabet, some numbers, and a couple of things about fingerspelling. We'll take care of all these things in this section, and before long you'll be ready to start signing.

# Chapter 5

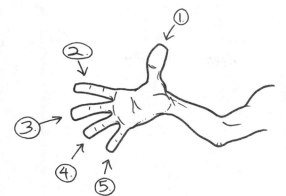

# The Four Parts of a Sign

## In This Chapter

➤ Learning the four components that make up a complete sign

➤ Mastering handshape is crucial to signing

➤ Discovering that it's not only what you sign, but where, that counts

➤ Altering your hand movement can change the meaning of a sign

➤ Remembering that palm position counts, too

➤ Putting the parts together and starting to sign

Sign language is lively, fun, and expressive. Native users are often playful with their language and take liberties when using it—much like speaking people enjoy saying certain words because they like how they sound, or using puns or plays on words.

Once you get really good at signing, you too will be able to play with the language. For now, though, you need to be careful and pay attention to details.

In this chapter we'll learn about four components that are used to form complete signs. We'll see how each one is important and necessary.

# The Main Components

Sign language has four components that together characterize a sign. Change any one of the components, and you may change whatever sign you're making into something completely different.

**A Good Sign**

If you're interested in an in-depth look at the linguistics of sign language, consider reading Stokoe's book *Sign Language Structure*. It's a scholarly work that can give you a great understanding of how sign language is put together, and what distinguishes it as a language in its own right. First published in 1960, the work has been reissued by Linstok Press in Silver Spring, Maryland.

The four parts of a sign are:

➤ Handshape

➤ Signing area

➤ Hand movement

➤ Position of the palm

As we mentioned in Chapter 3, William Stokoe was the first to propose that sign language was not a pantomime, but a complex system of symbols, containing different and distinct parts. It took a while for Stokoe's theories to gain credibility, but today it is recognized that he was, indeed, correct in his assertions.

Now, let's look at each of these components and at how together, they make up signs.

# Is That a "B," a "5," or a "Claw"?

Handshapes, three of which are listed in the title of this section, are integral to sign language. Each sign is formed with the hands in a particular position, or handshape. Many handshapes correspond to the letters of the manual alphabet, which we'll get into more in Chapter 8. Handshapes can also correspond to number shapes, which we'll learn in Chapter 9. Letter and number shapes are not signs, they're handshapes used in making a sign.

This is a rather confusing point that is difficult for many beginning signers to understand. But finger spelling, which is a system of spelling out words using the manual alphabet, is a manual form of English. It is not sign language.

If you form the shape of the manual alphabet letter "B," you'll be conveying only a letter. But, if you form the shape of the manual alphabet letter "B" and combine it with the correct palm position, hand movement and signing area, you'll be making a sign.

The manual alphabet is extremely useful. It's used for finger spelling as well as handshapes. The manual alphabet, however, is an invented method used in communicating, not a natural language like ASL.

When you get to Chapter 10 and start using the illustrated portion of this book that shows you various signs, it will be very important to make sure you're using the proper handshape. We'll tell you what handshape is used in each sign, and you'll probably need to check it to make sure you've got it right. It's a good idea to study the handshapes illustrated in Chapters 5, 8, and 9 before starting on the dictionary in Part 3.

As we said, many handshapes are alphabet or number shapes. Some, however, are neither.

The sign for "airplane," or "to fly in an airplane," for instance, uses the "I Love You" or ILY handshape. That handshape, which gained notoriety when it appeared on a postage stamp, is palm out, thumb, little, and index fingers up, with the middle fingers bent. To sign "airplane," you turn your palm down and move your hand up, out, and slightly away from you two times. The hand moves away from you further, but only once, when signing "to fly in an airplane."

The following figures show you some of these handshapes that are different from the manual alphabet or number shapes. Many of these variations are based on letter or number shapes and are commonly used in ASL.

*I Love You handshape.*

*Index handshape— the most commonly used handshape in ASL.*

*Flattened F handshape.*

*Folded 3 handshape.*

*"C with Thumb and Forefinger" handshape.*

*"Slightly Folded 5" handshape.*

*"Bent L" handshape.*

*"1-i" handshape.*

**53**

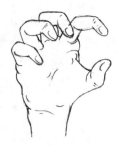

*"Flattened O" handshape.*

*"Closed 3" handshape.*

*"Claw 3" handshape.*

*"Claw" Handshape.*

Keep in mind that these handshapes don't represent all the variations that exist, but they give you an idea of some of those most commonly used.

# Location, Location, Location

It is very difficult to learn sign language from a book that has illustrations depicting only the hands when showing signs. Why? Because you won't know where to put your hands in relationship to your body, that's why.

**Signposts**

A good example of the importance of location when signing are the signs "summer" and "dry." These have the same handshape, movement, and position of the palm, but are located at different areas in relation to the body. "Summer" is signed at forehead level, while "dry" is signed at chin level. It well may be a dry summer, but you probably won't end up signing what you think you are if you mix up the location of the two signs.

The signing area is generally thought of as an imaginary rectangle. The area is shoulder width, extending from the top of the head to the waist. Nearly all signs are formed within the area, and for a logical reason. It's easiest to see signs when they're near the head or neck, as opposed to other areas of the body.

Signs used to be formed outside this imaginary rectangle more frequently than they are today. They've gradually moved into the signing area, making them easier to read.

Like real estate, it's location, location, location when learning sign language. You may have the same handshape, palm position, and movement, but completely change the meaning of a sign by where you are holding your hands.

Some signs would not make sense if performed in the wrong location. For instance, the sign for "napkin" is to move the open fingers of the right hand across the lips. This sign makes perfect sense because it is what you do with a napkin. But, if you were to sign "napkin" at chest level, it would be confusing, to say the least.

The sign for "stomach," you start with your right hand in a "bent B" handshape and tap above your waist. Get it? You tap on your stomach! Now, if you were to tap on your forehead with the same handshape, it wouldn't mean stomach, would it?

Say you're signing to your pal Harry about an operation your buddy Tom just had. It will be very clear to Harry that Tom had a knee operation if, when signing "operation," you sign it at your knee (in this case it's perfectly okay to leave the signing area—remember it's just imaginary). If you form the sign for "operation" at stomach level, Harry might think Tom had appendicitis, which isn't the case at all.

So, you'll need to pay close attention not only to *what* you're signing, but *where* you're signing it in relation to your body.

## Sign of the Times

A Deaf friend who teaches ASL laughs as she remembers some of the mistakes her students have made when learning to sign. One young man signed to her that he was going to have to miss class because he would be too busy "making out." He meant to sign "working." One of her favorite stories involves her husband, who is hearing, or Deaf impaired. While once watching her husband's clumsy attempts at signing, she saw him tell someone that she was his second "hamburger." What he meant to say, of course, was "second wife."

# Here, There, and Everywhere

Observe two people fluent in ASL as they carry on a conversation. The exchange will be a flurry of movement. Their bodies bend, facial expressions change constantly, and their hands seem to be constantly in motion.

Hand movement is not only an integral part of the energy and beauty of sign language, it can change the meaning of a sign. Direction, speed, and the intensity of hand movement are all important factors in signing.

## Stationary Signs

Some signs require no hand movement. These are called *stationary signs*. Some signs require movement by only one hand, while the other remains stationary. When movement is required, however, it is an integral part of a sign.

An example of a sign in which one hand is stationary while the other moves is "banana." The left index finger is pointed up while the right hand makes the motion of peeling a banana.

The meanings of some words change depending on the direction in which the hands are moved. If you sign "help" and pull the sign back toward your body, you're signing that you were helped or help was given to you. If you sign "help" and move your hands away from your body, you're signing that you gave help or helped somebody else. The same rule applies to words such as "give," "ask," and "tell."

## Speed and Intensity

**Signposts**
Saying that you love chocolate has a much different meaning than when you talk about your love for a spouse, child, or dear friend. You would demonstrate that difference by the tone of your voice, the look on your face, and your hand gestures and body language. The same is true with signing. It's all a matter of intensity.

**A Good Sign**
When signing in front of a group, it is wise to avoid finger spelling whenever possible. It is just too difficult to see finger spelling from a distance, and impossible to make it larger.

The speed at which a sign is given also communicates its meaning. If you're telling your child that as far as you're concerned, there's no big hurry to plan that sleep-over she wants to have, you'll sign "hurry" much differently than you would when telling her to "Hurry up, you're already 20 minutes late for school!"

Intensity is another important factor in hand movement and can affect the meaning of the sign. For instance, if you're signing to somebody about a rainstorm the previous day, you'll sign in a particular manner with a certain degree of intensity. If you're describing the tornado you got stuck in during your last trip to Kansas, however, your manner and level of intensity will be quite different!

Intensity is also reflected by facial expression, body language, and other factors that we'll discuss in Chapter 6. It's very important when signing "love," "beauty," "dislike," and other signs that can vary greatly in meaning. Intensity in signing can be compared to voice inflections and pitch levels in speaking.

If somebody is speaking before a group, he can speak loudly or turn on a microphone for amplification. Someone signing before a group can amplify her signs by increasing the size of the sign.

Signs intended for a group of people will extend past the body area, while signs used for conversing with just one or two others normally remain in the imaginary signing area.

# Up or Down, Right or Left?

The position of the palm is the last of the four basic parts of a sign. You might get everything else right, but if you turn your palm down when it should be up, you won't be signing what you want to. Palm position can completely change the meaning of a sign.

Now we've covered the four parts of a sign and have gotten you started on learning some handshapes. Hang in there. We'll soon learn the manual alphabet and the number handshapes. Then we'll put it all together and start learning some signs.

# The Least You Need to Know

➤ ASL has four distinct parts that make up each sign: handshape, signing area, hand movement, and position of the palm.

➤ Most but not all handshapes are the shapes for the manual alphabets or number shapes.

➤ The same handshape and movement can mean different things when signed in different locations.

➤ Nearly all signs are formed in the signing area, which is an imaginary rectangle extending shoulder width, from the waist to the top of the head.

➤ The speed, direction, and intensity of hand movement can change the tone and meaning of your sign.

➤ Palm position is important and must be learned properly.

# Chapter 6

# It's the Little Things That Make All the Difference

## In This Chapter

➤ Letting your dominant hand do the signing

➤ Using facial expressions with ASL

➤ Maintaining eye contact as much as possible

➤ Signing differences from person to person and place to place

While ASL is a language that uses sweeping hand movements and pronounced body language, it is also a language of subtleties. We've learned how a palm turned the wrong way can change the entire meaning of a sign. In addition, we've touched on the importance of facial expression and body position when signing.

We'll look more closely at some of these things in this chapter. We'll discuss which hand to use when signing, the importance of eye contact, and the changes that have occurred in ASL over the past few years. We'll look at how signing differs from person to person, and see that no two people will ever sign exactly alike.

# To Right, or Not to Right?

Just as there are right-handed and left-handed pitchers, tennis players, bowlers, and violinists, there are right-handed and left-handed signers.

Someone whose dominant hand is his right hand is almost always a right-handed signer, while a person whose left hand is the dominant one is almost always a left-handed signer. Of course, if you're a lefty who discovers it's more comfortable to sign right-handed, then go ahead and sign right-handed.

The dominant hand does most of the work. It forms the signs that require only one hand, and performs the main action for signs that require two hands. Some signs require that both hands move simultaneously, in which case the dominant hand idea doesn't apply.

The signs illustrated in this book are right-handed signs, but that doesn't mean that a left-handed signer can't learn from them. Just use your left hand as the dominant hand and form the same handshape, direction, and so on.

One thing for you ambidextrous readers to keep in mind is that, with certain exceptions in advanced signing, it's not acceptable to switch hands during the course of singing. If you start signing right-handed, then continue signing right-handed.

It's a good idea to decide early on whether you'll be a right- or left-handed signer. Try some finger spelling and some signs with each hand and see which feels more comfortable.

# In Your Face

Facial expression and eye contact are arguably as important when using ASL as the actual formation of signs. Fluent signers say they look at a person's face when signing, not his hands.

**A Good Sign**
When you have an opportunity to watch two fluent signers in action, observe carefully. More likely than not, your eyes will be drawn to the faces of the signers and you'll be fascinated by the range of expression used. The hands actually become secondary to the face.

## Facial Expression

Every language uses some facial expression, but ASL takes it to a different level. Facial expression in ASL not only conveys emotion or emphasis, it tells you a great deal about what kind of sentence or thought is being signed, and how it is organized. It actually becomes a tool of grammar in ASL.

Something as subtle as blinking the eyes can signal the type of phrase being signed. Eye blinks are used to signal conditional clauses, such as in the sentence, "If the auditorium was damaged in the storm, we'll hold the meeting somewhere else."

If eye blinks and several other facial indicators are not used when signing that sentence, the person receiving the information will not understand it. Without facial expression, the sentence likely would be understood as "The auditorium was damaged, we'll hold the meeting somewhere else."

**Signposts**
Some signs incorporate facial expressions and would not be complete without them. An example is "recent," which calls for the signer to raise his shoulders and stick out his lower lip.

In spoken language, a person talking before a group or reading aloud normally waits until the end of a clause or phrase to take a breath. For instance, former President Grover Cleveland said in 1886 during a message to the American people, "When more of the people's sustenance is exacted through the form of taxation than is necessary to meet the just obligations of government and expenses of its economical administration, such exaction becomes ruthless extortion and a violation of the fundamental principles of a free government."

It is safe to assume, wouldn't you agree, that Grover couldn't wait to take a big breath after the clause ending with economical administration. If he had been signing, he would properly have indicated the end of that clause with an eye blink.

Another use of facial expression is to indicate not only that a question is being asked, but the type of question it is. A yes or no question is accompanied with raised eyebrows. When asking a who, what, when, where, or why question, the eyebrows are kept lowered, and a frown appears on the face.

Speaking people use tone and volume to put meaning in their words. Picture this: Another person is watching you perform a task at home. Say you're painting the woodwork around the fireplace. You've worked carefully and everything looks great. "Oh, that's really a great job," the person says admiringly.

Or, you've been particularly sloppy with this job, and paint is all over the carpet and the fireplace bricks. "Oh, that's really a great job," the person says scornfully.

You get the point. Same words, but different emphasis and tone. In one case you're a household hero, in the other case you'd better start looking for someplace else to hang out that evening.

Signing people do the same thing, but with facial expression. The person viewing the paint job in the first scenario would sign the equivalent of "Oh, that's really a great job," while assuming a pleasant facial expression. He might nod his head and keep his face relaxed and smiling. You, the painter, can prepare for a pleasant evening.

The person in the second scenario, however, would look quite different while signing the equivalent of "Oh, that's really a great job." He might squeeze his eyebrows together and shake his head from side to side. He might purse his lips and perhaps he would suck in his breath. These would be your cues to stick a change of clothes in a backpack and go find a friend with some room to spare.

Facial expression not only conveys emotion, it conveys the *degree* of emotion. You might sign "sorry" to a friend who tells you he has the sniffles with a fairly bland look on your face. I mean, it's too bad he's not feeling great, but, come on, it's just a cold. When you sign "sorry" to a friend who tells you his mother just died, however, you'll look completely different. This is terrible news, and your face will respond with an extremely sad look, brows drawn up and mouth in a frown.

Squinting your eyes while making a sign adds emphasis. It's like adding very in front of a word when speaking. Squinting while signing that someone is pretty indicates a real knockout. Squinting while signing that someone is tall indicates NBA material. You get the idea.

Some facial expressions are universal. They are used pretty much in the same way in all languages, manual and oral. Even squinting the eyes applies somewhat to spoken language. Someone talking about the NBA candidate is likely to narrow his eyes while saying "He's soooooo tall!"

Another universal expression is surprise. Eyes and mouth opened wide with the eyebrows raised means surprise almost everywhere. Narrowed eyes and pursed lips signify anger among most people, and joy is expressed nearly universally with smiles and laughter—and sometimes tears.

Even small children learn to recognize these expressions, which are used frequently in cartoons and kids' books. Deaf people, too, often use these common facial expressions when telling a story or conversing with friend. They may be exaggerated for effect or used conservatively, but they convey the same meaning in sign as in nearly every other language.

### Sign of the Times

In addition to thrilling athletic competition, the Olympics provide great opportunity to view the facial expressions of people from many countries and cultures. Few English-speaking people could understand what Japan's Hiroyasu Shimizu was saying just after he won a gold medal in the 500-meter speedskating event during the 1998 Winter Olympics. People watching around the world, though, felt his joy by watching his face and body language. Smiles, laughter, tears, bows, and upraised arms expressed his joy and gratitude.

Deaf people who use sign language are very good at recognizing and interpreting facial expression. They normally are attuned to slight variations of expression and perceptive to the changes. Interestingly, studies have shown that Deaf children who learn sign language at a very young age grow up with have far better visual perception overall than hearing children.

Someone who is speaking can get away with a bland expression and little voice inflection, because his words can adequately express his thoughts. Someone signing, however, does not have that option. Sign language without facial expression is more like mere hand motions than language. It simply doesn't work well at all, and your signing may not be understood.

# Eye Contact

Eye contact in sign language is also extremely important. As we said earlier, it is a natural tendency to look at the face of a person who is signing. Your eyes are naturally drawn there, and many people find it difficult to break eye contact. Again, as our friend Martha Stewart would say, "it's a good thing." It is considered rude and disrespectful to look away when someone is signing.

The rules of etiquette differ between signed and spoken language. In spoken conversation, a person is considered a good listener if she watches the person who is speaking and gives signs that she really hears what's being said. She may nod occasionally, indicating that she is listening intently to the story of how Arthur broke up with Eleanor because he's smitten with that new secretary with the short skirt. She might make small sounds to indicate she's heard the speaker say that Eleanor is so upset about Arthur that she's seeing her therapist three times a week and has completely stopped going to the gym. She is acknowledging the conversation and the person who is speaking.

A not-so-good listener, or someone who has been subjected too many times to Aunt Ethel's stories of her gall bladder surgery, often appears to be distracted. He may look at his watch, examine his fingernails, and respond to noises in other parts of the room. He might be listening to Aunt Ethel and even answering her, but he is not giving her his undivided attention. Some people might say he's being rude, but he can still be involved in the conversation.

Not so, however, in a signed conversation. Breaking eye contact with someone who is signing to you is akin to sticking your fingers into your ears when somebody is talking to you. It indicates both a lack of interest and a lack of respect for the signer.

There are exceptions, of course. If you smell something funny and catch a glimpse of flames out of the corner of your eye, it would be foolhardy to stay put for fear of offending Josh by breaking eye contact before he finishes the story of how he's just gotten word of his third promotion in less than a year. You have to assume that Josh will understand the urgency of such a situation and overlook your rudeness.

If you're just tired of listening to Josh's stories, however, and more than a little annoyed because he's now got a fancy office and his own secretary (maybe even that one with the short skirt) and you're still in the cubbyhole back by the men's room, then it is not acceptable for you to be deliberately rude and break eye contact.

Josh, on the other hand, is free to break eye contact as he signs. He might close his eyes as he signs to emphasize something (perhaps having to do with his new secretary), or look at something in order to call attention to it as part of the conversation. In this way, he is using his eyes as a substitute for a pointed finger, which is the most common way to refer to something that has already been mentioned.

Sometimes signers break and then reestablish eye contact with the person receiving the conversation to indicate that they do not wish to be interrupted.

**Warning Sign**
Breaking eye contact during signing is considered very rude among Deaf people, but it's not the only action that is frowned upon in Deaf culture. For reasons that aren't completely clear, it is considered bad form to step out to make a phone call or use the bathroom without giving an explanation. It also is considered rude to suddenly leave a gathering.

It is customary for the person receiving sign language to wait until the signer looks at him before he starts a turn at signing. If Josh is really enjoying telling his story of his promotion and new secretary, he may avoid looking at you because he's not ready to end his turn at signing.

This is not all to say that sign language is an exact language, with rules that are set in stone. A group of Deaf people who get together at a club or someone's home will not sit in an orderly fashion, signing one at a time while the rest of the group maintains constant eye contact.

ASL is used as it was intended to be used—for real, effective conversation. When a group of people begin signing all at once, it will eventually become impossible to understand what is being communicated. The same thing happens when a group of people all start speaking at once.

## Body Language

Like facial expression, body language plays a big part in sign language. If someone is signing that she's tired, she'll slump while making the sign. Someone expressing great love for another will cross her hands across her chest and may rock back and forth to indicate intensity.

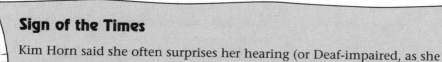

### Sign of the Times

Kim Horn said she often surprises her hearing (or Deaf-impaired, as she jokingly calls him) husband by making predictions about their friends. "We'll be on our way home from a party and I'll tell Tom that so-and-so aren't getting along," Kim says. "He won't believe me, but six months later they'll be divorced." She says that she and other ASL users are more attuned to body language than hearing people because they're used to watching for it in their language. "Plus," Kim says, "Deaf people are always watching other people and trying to figure out what's going on!"

Body language, facial expression, eye contact, and movement must all be considered and coordinated when signing. The use of these tools might seem exaggerated and somewhat odd at first, but eventually you'll see that they, along with the signs, are natural expressions of your thoughts.

## Are We Signing the Same Language Here?

Because no two people are alike, no two people will sign in exactly the same way. You can study sign language with the same teacher for years, learning all the signs exactly as presented and copying the teacher's every move. But, as soon as you get comfortable with signing on your own, your use of ASL will become individualized. You'll develop your own personal style of signing and nobody else will do it quite the same way you do.

Many of these differences in style are due to physical variations. Some people are very limber and can move quickly. Everything works together the way it should—like a well-made machine. Fingers fly, arms move rhythmically up and down, the body bends and turns.

But what about someone who suffers from arthritis or whose movement is otherwise restricted? It's common sense to realize that if it hurts to move your fingers and hands, your movements will be slower and less fluid than they would be otherwise. Elderly people may find it becomes increasingly difficult to use sign language due to arthritis and other conditions.

### Signposts
Some research indicates that practicing and using finger spelling can actually slow down the advances of arthritis in the fingers.

Other physical attributes can also affect signing. Height, weight, and body proportion will affect the way you sign, giving you a style all your own.

**A Good Sign**
A hearing woman who works closely with Deaf people every day said she is often teased about her *accent*. A Southern native now living in the Northeast, she gets a lot of good-natured kidding about her style of sign language. She never takes the teasing seriously because it's all given in fun.

Personal differences in signing are no different from personal differences in speaking. Some people speak slowly, some quickly. Some lisp or have other peculiarities. Usually, we can all manage to make ourselves understood and understand others.

We've already mentioned in Chapter 3 that there are regional variations of ASL. Some of these are pronounced and can make it difficult for two signing people to understand each other. Generally, Deaf people are accepting of these differences and don't place values on them. They merely acknowledge them for what they are— differences.

## Sign Variation

Certain signs tend to vary more than others. Signs for holidays vary greatly from region to region. It is thought that this is due to children in Deaf residential schools who invented signs for Christmas, Easter, Valentine's Day, and other holidays to represent something that was special to them about the day. If kids at one school received chocolate on Valentine's Day, for instance, the sign they invented might reflect that gift. It could be something completely different, though, for the children who observed Valentine's Day in a different manner.

One thing is certain—American signs reflect American culture. It is intriguing to begin to understand the origins of signs. The sign for "store," for instance, reflects something particular about stores as viewed in American culture.

It used to be, and still is in many cases, that most stores had bells above their doors so that shopkeepers would be alerted when customers entered. The ASL sign for store, hands in the "O" handshape, held at shoulder level with the wrist rotating out two times, is indicative of ringing bells.

In Jamaica, the sign for "store," formed with the hands held above the head, reflects the cultural tradition of carrying a basket on the head to and from a store.

Although there is not yet a formalized international sign language, there are some signs that seem to be widely accepted as international; for example, the proper names of countries. Deaf people in Belgium have their own sign for their country, as do Deaf people in other countries. But people in other countries do not use the same sign for Belgium that Belgians do. They have their own signs for Belgium. It is becoming more acceptable and politically correct, however (if nothing else, the '90s will be remembered as being the era of political correctness) to use the sign that is the choice of the people of a particular country.

There is a movement underway to develop an international sign language called Gestuno, which is a language of signs chosen by an international committee. These signs are not invented signs, but taken from existing sign languages. It is not known whether Gestuno will ever become widely used, and there is ongoing debate over the credibility of such a language.

It's important to recognize that there are variations in sign language and to be flexible. Don't assume you're doing it right—or wrong—because someone is signing in a manner different than yours. Keep in mind that physical differences as well as regional and cultural variations can, and do, result in a broad spectrum of signing styles. After a while you'll develop your own style and become comfortable with the styles of others.

## Get With It, Mom

What was hip to one generation is awesome to another, and cool to those somewhere in between. Men used to wear trousers, but today men (and women) wear pants. Listening to the Victrola used to be a pleasurable pastime. Today's music lovers play CDs.

Just as words change, signs change. Old signs become obsolete and die out and are replaced by new ones. Because sign language is a living, evolving language, there are constant changes to it.

These changes come from necessity. Ten years ago there was no widely recognized sign for fax or Internet, because very few people had ever heard of these things. Now there are common signs for these words. Changes that occur in the world will always be reflected in language—both signed and spoken.

## The Least You Need to Know

➤ ASL is full of subtleties and intricacies that will become more apparent as you learn more about the language.

➤ Right-handed or left-handed signing is fine, but it's not appropriate to switch back and forth.

➤ ASL is highly dependent on facial expression and body language.

➤ Looking away from someone who is signing is rude and disrespectful.

➤ Differences in physical attributes and personality mean that no two people will sign exactly alike.

➤ New signs emerge to replace ones that are no longer useful, much the same as in spoken language.

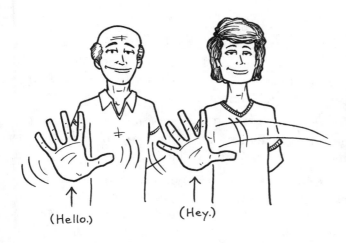

(Hello.)  (Hey.)

# Chapter 7

# Variations On a Basic Sign

## In This Chapter

➤ Indicating gender when signing

➤ Using the person marker to indicate occupation or nationality

➤ Using natural or iconic signs as they appear in ASL

➤ Initializing and modifying signs as a means of clarification

➤ Applying possessives and plurals

Fluent users of ASL know and understand the many nuances of the language. Forming plurals and possessives, clarifying signs, and clearly indicating meaning in different ways is done naturally and easily.

For those just learning the language, however, these things will require some explanation and practice. In this chapter, we'll have a look at some issues like establishing gender, using natural or iconic signs, and using the person marker. These are small, but important aspects of signing that will help make your use of the language clear and understandable.

# Gender Rules

ASL is an efficient language. It takes less time for a good signer to tell a story in ASL than it does for a person speaking English to tell the same story.

**Signposts**
It takes three words in English to tell your friend that you'll follow him as he pulls out in front of you in his car. One quick sign will do the same in ASL.

One example of ASL's efficiency is found in how gender is represented. Many signs have a built-in gender; that is, there is male or female incorporated in the sign.

How is this done? Gender is indicated by the location at which a sign is made. Typically, male signs are located on the upper part of the face, while female signs are located on the lower part of the face.

Imagine a line drawn horizontally across the face. The gender signing area is split just about evenly in half—from the top of the forehead to the bottom of the chin.

Indicating gender with location comes in handy when signing. If you're signing something about your cousin, for instance, the person you're communicating with knows whether your cousin is a man or a woman without having to ask. "Cousin" has the same handshape, palm orientation, and hand movement. The only difference is where the sign is made. The same is true for "grandmother/grandfather," "stepmother/stepfather," and "brother/sister."

These gender-indicative signs are similar to words in Spanish or other Romance languages. In Spanish, for example, a boy child is "muchacho," while a girl is "muchacha." A subtle difference, but one that clearly tells you what's what.

# Signs For All People

**A Good Sign**
To form the person marker, you start with both open hands (fingers held straight out) in front of you at about chest level with the palms facing each other. Move your hands straight down in front of your body.

Obviously, people are the topic of many, many conversations, whether signed or spoken. Think about all conversations you hold during a day, and then consider how many of those conversations are about people.

You might start off in the morning by commenting that the paper boy was late. Then you run through your plans for the day, which include meeting with your child's teacher, lunch with your friend Joanie, and a meeting with your boss about that project you're working on. See? You've already talked about the paper boy, your kid's teacher, Joanie, and your boss. All that people conversation, and you haven't even had your breakfast yet!

Let's make this a bit clearer. Say your first stop for the day is a meeting with your son's teacher, so let's look at the sign for "teacher":

➤ Make the sign for "teach" by moving your hands, with your thumbs touching the flattened fingers of each hand, forward from near the temple (See illustration in Chapter 12.)

➤ Add the person marker.

Adding the person marker tells the recipient of your conversation that you're talking about a person who teaches—a teacher. The same idea applies to many professions: writers, photographers, pilots, chefs, students, actors and actresses, soldiers, sailors, thieves, secretaries, treasurers, dancers, and so on.

The person marker is not just for identifying occupations, though. It is also used when signing "neighbor" and in identifying nationalities. To sign a nationality, you make the country's sign, and then add the person marker, indicating you are talking about a Frenchman and not France.

As you get more comfortable with signing, you'll learn to use the person marker freely. Go ahead! But be careful that you don't mistakenly cause confusion by adding it to something that is not clear. If you sign "skate" and add the person marker, everyone will know that the subject of your conversation is a skater. If you sign "tree" and add the person marker, however, you might generate some raised eyebrows. What would that mean? Someone who trims trees? Someone who loves trees? Someone who plants trees? Someone who climbs trees? You get the point!

# Compound Signs

Person markers are one way to form compound signs, which are two or more signs combined to form a separate sign ("teach" and "person" = "teacher"). There are other kinds of compound signs, as well. Compound signs are common in ASL, as in English. You will see numerous compound signs when you start using the dictionary later in this book.

Compound signs break down into two or more signs that have been combined to form a separate sign. Common compound signs are those with "room" as one of signs. There is a sign for "room" that can be used on its own to indicate any old kind of room. Or, "room" can be combined with other signs to indicate a particular kind of room, such as a bedroom, ballroom, sitting room, or drawing room.

Other kinds of compound signs that take a little more work to figure out. For instance, the sign for "snow" is actually two signs—the sign for "white" and the sign for "(soft) rain." It makes perfect sense, but the concept requires a bit of thought when you first encounter it.

# Could It Mean Anything Else?

Natural or *iconic signs* are very interesting and a boon to the beginning signer because they're easy to learn and remember. They're also a lot of fun. Iconic signs are the easiest to read and remember because they are signs that look like the object or the movement of the object that you are signing.

We hope you understand by now that ASL is by no means iconography, or picture drawing. If it were, almost anyone would be able to watch two people using ASL and know what was being communicated—as if they were playing charades. If you haven't had a chance to observe fluent signers, try to arrange for the opportunity. You'll quickly see that you can't depend on iconicity to clue you in on what the signers are communicating.

ASL does contain some natural or iconic signs but the complexity and structure that characterize it give the language far deeper depth than a pictorial language would have. *Iconicity* in signed language has been compared to onomatopoeia (remember *that* word from grammar class?) in spoken language. In case you've forgotten, onomatopoeia refers to a word that sounds like what it describes. "Buzz," "zip," "hiss," "whoosh," "swish," and "zoom" are some examples. Some linguists have suggested that the first spoken words were all onomatopoetic. That doesn't discredit spoken language in any way, just as iconic signs don't discredit sign language.

Studies have shown that many hearing, non-signing people think ASL is more iconic than it really is. But tests have shown that when non-signers are asked to identify the meanings of commonly used signs that might be considered somewhat iconic, most of them can't.

The results are equally poor on multiple-choice tests, during which non-hearing signers are shown signs and given choices of what the signs might mean. The participants answered correctly only about 20 percent of the time, which is about what you'd expect if they were guessing at the answers. Non-signers, however, tend to have better success identifying the origin of signs when they know what the English translation is.

The sign for "tea," for instance, looks like the action of dipping a tea bag into a cup. Non-signers who see this sign and are told that it means "tea" are likely to be able to figure out the association. The same is true with the sign for "toothbrush," which is made by moving your index finger back and forth in front of your mouth, while wiggling the finger up and down. It's clearly the motion of tooth-brushing and easy to identify.

Other examples of iconic signs include:

➤ "Pet," as in to pet a dog. The right hand moves over the left in a petting motion.

➤ "Smile." Fingertips start at the corners of the mouth, then pull up as if stretching the mouth into a smile.

➤ "Jump." The fingers of the right hand "hop" up and down on the outstretched palm of the left hand.

➤ "Rainbow." The fingers, held slightly apart, follow the shape and indicate the division of colors of a rainbow.

➤ "Listen." The hand is raised to the ear.

ASL uses iconicity in another interesting way to indicate space. We're not talking about *space* as in the vast universe around us into which rockets are launched, but the space and time around us, as indicated by words such as deep, high, future, past, behind, and forward.

> **Signposts**
> Signs for sports tend to be very iconic. "Baseball" is signed by making the motion of holding a baseball bat. "Basketball" is signed by making the motion of holding a basketball and throwing a chest pass. "Tennis," "golf," "bowling," and "boxing" are also extremely iconic signs that mime the actions used in the particular sports.

While these concepts must be assigned words in spoken language, they can be incorporated into an ASL sign. If Fred is telling Carol that the anniversary celebration will be in 2010, he's likely to sign the event out in front of his body. If he's signing about the anniversary celebration next week, the sign will be made closer to his body. And if he's signing about the celebration held two years ago, he may lean back or sign slightly behind his shoulder.

Another example of iconicity in ASL is how signs that indicate *good* things are made differently than those that indicate *bad* things. Signs such as those for "discouraged," "depressed," "fear," "sorrow," and "troubled" use downward motions, while signs for "proud," "thrilled," "excited," and "cheerful" use upward motions.

All these iconic uses give clues to the nature of signing and what is being signed. They certainly don't substitute for a thorough knowledge of the language, but can be used as a learning tool to make signing and understanding some signs a little easier.

# A Bit Of Clarification, Please

Natural signs are nice, but many, many ASL signs are lacking in iconic value. This being the 90s, we'll say these signs are *iconographically challenged*. ASL has a solution to iconographically challenged signs, however: *initialized signs*.

Initialized signs are those in which the handshape, used to form a sign, is the shape of the first letter of the corresponding English word. We mentioned in Chapter 5 that many ASL handshapes are those of the American Manual Alphabet (AMA) and of numbers. Then we showed you some handshapes that are neither, but which are also used in ASL.

When discussing initialized signs, we're talking about using the AMA handshapes to indicate the initial letter of the word being signed. Initializing a sign is useful in ASL to help distinguish between signs that are similar but that have different meanings.

Consider the signs for "family," "team," "group," "class," "department," and "organization." The signs share the same locations, movements, and palm orientations. The only difference is the handshapes, which vary according to the initial letter of each word. "Family" is signed with an "F" handshape, "team" with a "T" handshape, "group" with a "G" handshape, and so on.

Other examples of initialized signs are "music" and "poetry" and "honor" and "respect." You can see that the initialized signs all have meanings that are related, but different.

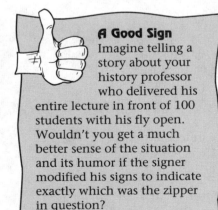

**Warning Sign**
Some sign language teachers and experts complain that initialized signs are used too frequently, when they're really not necessary. Many initialized signs are not pure ASL, they say, but an evolution of the root ASL sign. Initialized signs are fine when used properly, but should not be overused.

## Modified Signs

As with initialized signs, *modified signs* occur when the signer intentionally changes the way a sign is made in order to clarify its meaning. Modified signs help to make the meaning of the sign more specific.

A good example is the sign for "zipper." "Zip, zip your zipper, up to your chin…" is a song you may have learned in kindergarten. The generic sign for "zipper" uses the same zipping motion, up and down from waist to chin. But what if you're talking about zip, zipping the zipper of your jeans? Or your boot? Or your purse? Well, you could still indicate zipping on your chest, but it wouldn't be very specific. Instead, zipping your jeans zipper is signed at the part of your body where your jeans zipper is located, zipping your boot zipper is signed low, and zipping your purse zipper is signed in front of you.

**A Good Sign**
Imagine telling a story about your history professor who delivered his entire lecture in front of 100 students with his fly open. Wouldn't you get a much better sense of the situation and its humor if the signer modified his signs to indicate exactly which was the zipper in question?

The sign for "open" is one that is often modified. The generic sign for "open" is similar to opening a book, or pulling back both sides of a container at one time. But what about opening a window? Or opening your mouth to speak? Or opening the door? The same applies to "close," "build," "climb," "wash," and many other words.

Modified signs take some practice, but they're a valuable and enriching part of sign language. Be aware of the context in which you're using signs, and consider how modifying a sign might make your meaning more clear.

# Whose Car? Or Is It Cars?

How does a signer indicate ownership? How does a singer indicate more than one of something? These are questions we'll consider in the following sections.

## Possession

Your friend Sally just had a baby and you're thrilled! You've gotten all the details from Sally's husband about Baby Robbie, the eight-pound-looks-just-like-his-dad addition to the family. Naturally, you want to tell everyone at the luncheon you're going to this afternoon all about the good news. Just how will you do that?

When you tell your friends that Sally had her baby, point toward a spot when you first refer to Sally. That spot will represent Sally during the entire conversation. This is called *indexing* and it establishes a location for Sally. Then, when referring to Sally, point to the established location and use the possessive sign, which is an open palm toward Sally's established location. Because you established a location for Sally when you first mentioned her, other signers will understand that you're signing about Sally whenever you point to that location.

> **Signposts**
> Indexing is another example of the efficiency of ASL. Once a location for a person or thing is established, you merely point at it to indicate who or what you're talking about. It's much quicker and easier to point than to keep saying "my Great-Uncle Oliver."

## Plurals

English words are usually made plural by adding an "s" or by changing the word, such as "goose" to "geese." In ASL, though, there are different ways to indicate plurals. You can make a noun plural by signing in front of it any of the qualifiers that indicate more than one. These qualifiers include "many," "all," "several," "some," and "both." So, if you sign "many" and then "bird," your ornithologist friends will know you're talking about a flock of birds instead of one lonely wood thrush at your bird feeder.

Another way of pluralizing in ASL is by repetition. Simply make the sign two or more times to indicate more than one of an object. Repeating a sign is often used to indicate an action that is performed several times. For instance, if you were running around bird-watching all day long, you'd repeat the sign to tell people about your extended activity.

You can also pluralize by pointing. When you're telling your card club about the flock of blue jays that chased the nuthatches from the bird feeder this morning, you can sign "bird" and then point at imaginary locations where the birds were. A sweeping motion with your hand will also indicate a group of something. Or you can show plurality by using space to indicate a "row of" trees or a "row of" birds sitting on a wire.

These all are common and practical methods of forming plurals in ASL. It doesn't really matter which method you use, and you'll probably use all of them as you become more adept at signing. You'll quickly learn which feels most comfortable in a particular conversation.

## The Least You Need to Know

➤ Gender is indicated by the part of the face on which the sign is made. Male signs are made on the upper part of the face, while female signs are made on the lower part.

➤ A person marker is extremely useful in identifying occupation and nationality.

➤ Some ASL signs are natural or iconic signs. These signs are helpful to beginning signers because they're easy to form and to remember.

➤ Initialized signs are formed when the signer uses the handshape of the first letter of the corresponding English word to indicate the sign being made.

➤ Modified signs are formed when the signer changes the way in which a sign is made in order to change the meaning of the sign.

➤ Possessives are indicated by an open palm, directed toward an indexed position. An index position establishes a location for the person or thing you're referring to.

➤ Plurals are indicated by using qualifiers, repetition, or by pointing.

# Chapter 8

# ABCs and So Forth

## In This Chapter

➤ Learning the American Manual Alphabet

➤ Realizing there are many manual alphabets found throughout the world

➤ Learning how finger spelling is different than sign language

➤ Understanding how much finger spelling is enough

➤ Practicing is the way to improve finger spelling

Remember learning the ABCs when you were in preschool or the early elementary grades? First, you probably learned the ABC song. Then you learned to recognize the letters, and finally to write them. With that out of the way, you were well on your way to reading.

A similar process will occur as you learn ASL. There's no alphabet song, but you're going to learn to recognize the letters of the American Manual Alphabet and to form those letters with your hands. It will take some practice, just like it did way back in elementary school. But, once you've memorized the manual alphabet, which also serves as many of the ASL handshapes, you'll be well on your way to signing. Let's get started.

# The American Manual Alphabet

The American Manual Alphabet contains 26 handshapes that correspond to the letters of the English alphabet. It is used for finger spelling, a system of communication that involves spelling out words in an alphabetical language.

Finger spelling can be used by itself, but it's most often used in conjunction with sign language to spell out proper names and technical words. It is cumbersome and time consuming to use as a means of communication by itself. The average finger spelling rate is about 60 words per minute, which is only about 40 percent as fast as the normal rate of speaking.

People who are deaf and blind will often use finger spelling on its own. One makes handshapes and movements on the palm of the deaf, blind person receiving the message.

Some of the handshapes are the exact shapes of the printed block letter they represent and are easy to remember. Some are a bit trickier. You've already learned that a handshape is not a sign, but a tool invented for use in communication. Manual alphabets are not natural languages, but useful additions to those languages. The handshapes are relatively easy and can be learned in just a few hours. As we discussed in Chapter 4, however, much practice will be necessary before you'll be fully comfortable and proficient in finger spelling.

> **A Good Sign**
> People who have studied these sorts of things report that the manner in which a person naturally forms the "X" handshape is affected by heredity, just like the color of your eyes or how tall you are.

Use the practice tips in Chapter 4, and try to find a friend to practice with. And remember: Try to relax and enjoy yourself.

The handshapes of the American Manual Alphabet, as illustrated here, are shown as they would appear to the person reading them.

A

B

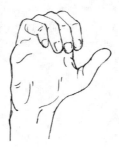

C

D

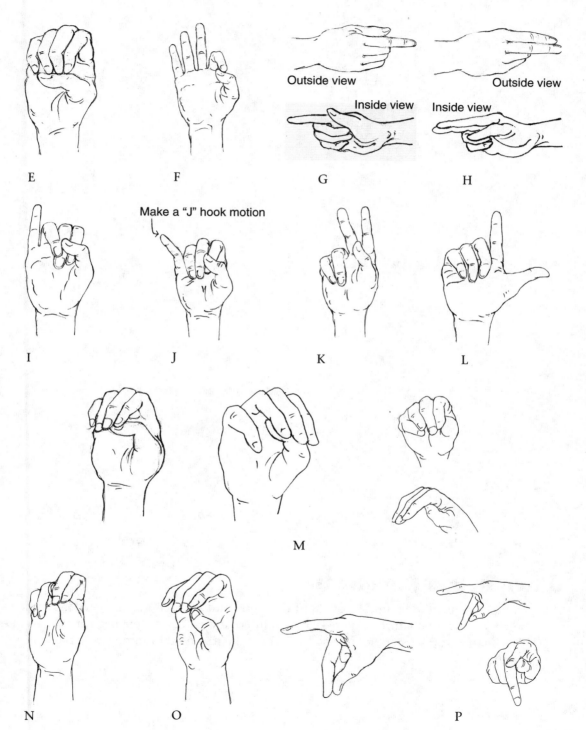

E

F

G

Outside view

Inside view

H

Outside view

Inside view

I

J

Make a "J" hook motion

K

L

M

N

O

P

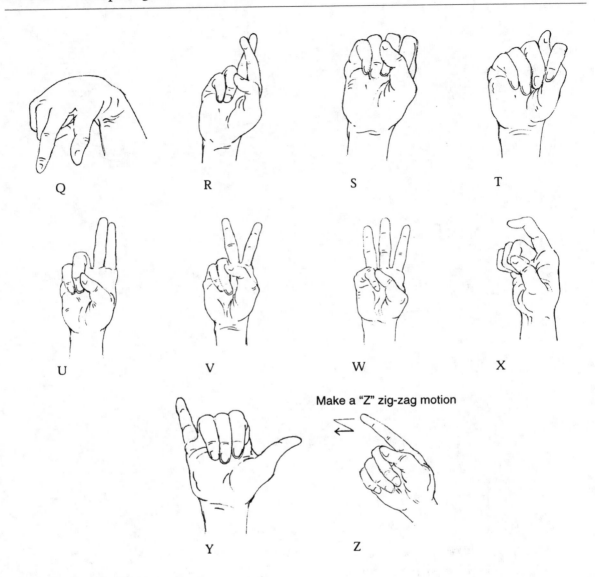

Q

R

S

T

U

V

W

X

Make a "Z" zig-zag motion

Y

Z

# Other Signed Alphabets

Manual alphabets are found throughout the world and are used in the signed languages of many different countries. There is also an international hand alphabet, introduced in 1975 by the World Federation of the Deaf. It is primarily used in some Scandinavian countries.

**Sign of the Times**

Although England and the United States use the same basic spoken and written languages, their manual alphabets vary greatly. In fact, most American signers, even fluent signers, can't read the British manual alphabet. Why? It uses two hands to form letters and is completely different from the American manual alphabet.

The earliest manual alphabet is thought to have been developed in the 1500s by Pedro Ponce de Leon, and first published in 1620 by Juan Pablo Bonet. Remnants of that first manual alphabet are still evident today in many one-handed alphabets used throughout the world.

Even countries that do not use the Latin alphabet—on which Bonet's system was based—have been influenced by the original manual alphabet. Israel, which uses the Hebrew alphabet, and Russia, which uses the Cyrillic alphabet, have manual alphabets that stem from Bonet's system.

There are exceptions to those countries influenced by Bonet's alphabet, however. In addition to Britain's two-handed system, there is the Swedish manual alphabet, which was developed independently of Bonet's system by Per Borg. It is the parent of the manual alphabets used today in Sweden and also in Portugal.

Countries without written alphabet systems, such as China and Japan, also have manual alphabets. In China, where a manual alphabet is just being developed, most Deaf people draw the outlines of Chinese characters in the air or into the palm of the person with whom they're communicating.

The Japanese finger spelling system is based on syllables instead of single sounds.

# When to Use Finger Spelling (and When Not to)

You already know there's not a corresponding sign for every English word. Names, brand names, and some very specific objects, thoughts, and actions are generally not signed, but finger spelled. For example, there's a sign for "ketchup," but "Heinz" would be finger spelled. The same is true for "coffee"/"Folgers," "car"/"Oldsmobile," "magazine"/"*Good Housekeeping*," and so on.

Signers normally finger spell the name of a person they're first meeting, or on first reference to a person during a conversation. People who sign together often, however—friends and family—usually give each other sign names that are easier to use than finger spelling the name would be.

In some families of Deaf people, all members are given a name with a common element to signify family unity. All the name signs might be located on the chin, for instance. The handshapes would be different, but the location the same.

Sometimes there is a lag period between the time when something new comes into use (such as a computer or other high-tech equipment) and the time when a common sign for it appears. "Internet" is an example of such a word. Finger spelling would be used to identify the product until a common sign becomes available.

You should use finger spelling for the following:

➤ Proper names of people

➤ Proper names of animals

➤ Titles of movies, books, magazines, etc.

➤ Brand names (with a few exceptions)

➤ Municipal names such as cities, counties, and townships (remember that many countries and some larger cities have signed names)

If there is a sign for a word, it's generally better to use the sign than to finger spell. Finger spelling slows down the signing process and the person you're signing to can become impatient. As an ASL beginner, however, it's understandable if you fall back on finger spelling when you forget a sign.

# Doing It Right

We gave you some ideas in Chapter 4 of good ways to practice finger spelling. Finger spelling the names of streets while you're in your car, or the newspaper headlines as you eat your cereal, will increase your familiarity with finger spelling as well as your speed.

Here are some other tips for becoming a proficient finger speller:

➤ Keep your hand in one place, near shoulder height, with the elbow down.

➤ Keep your arm reasonably stationary. Your hand, wrist, and sometimes your forearm move, but the arm does not move up and down or from side to side.

➤ Pause for just a second between finger spelled words, but not between letters.

➤ Try to make your finger spelling fluid, not jerky. This will come in time.

➤ Keep your palm turned toward the receiver (except in a few cases).

Finger spelling is like many other skills. Once you've accomplished it, you'll wonder what the big deal was. But, when you're first starting, you think you'll never get there. So, hang in there and practice, practice, practice.

# The Least You Need to Know

➤ The American Manual Alphabet contains 26 handshapes. Each handshape corresponds to a letter of written English.

➤ There are many manual alphabets throughout the world. Most of them trace their origins to the one recorded in 1620 by Juan Pablo Bonet.

➤ Finger spell most names of people and animals; brand names; titles of books, plays and movies; and the names of cities, counties, states, and schools.

➤ Don't finger spell if there is a sign you can use instead. Finger spelling slows down the signing process.

➤ There are some guidelines to consider when finger spelling such as hand position, timing, and arm movement.

# 1-2-3s

Numbers are as important in ASL as they are in spoken English. Think of how many times in a day we use them. We ask for six apples at the market or two napkins at the fast-food place. We count $40 in our wallets or six pieces of mail at our doors.

We tell our addresses to the delivery people, and recite our credit-card numbers to reserve hotel rooms, or order shoes from catalogs. We ask for $15 worth of gas and two quarts of oil. We measure out one and one-half cups of milk for the pudding and make six hamburgers for dinner.

We use numbers all the time, and their use is just as frequent in sign language. That means we'd better learn about numbers and how they're used in various situations. Let's have a look.

# Numbers From 1–9

You're going to love these! The handshapes for the numbers one through nine are easy to learn and to remember. In fact, you probably already use some of them. The five-year-old next door uses them all the time.

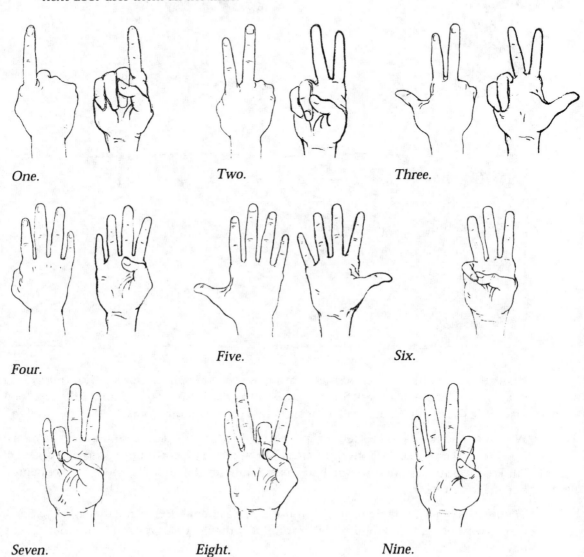

One.

Two.

Three.

Four.

Five.

Six.

Seven.

Eight.

Nine.

There's something you need to know about these 1–9 number handshapes. In addition to representing numerals, they're also used in a variety of signs. For instance, the sign for "knife," which we'll learn when we get to Chapter 14, our food-related chapter, is made with both hands in the "1" handshape.

We'll be seeing these handshapes a lot as we get into the signing dictionary. Once you've practiced these a few times, we'll move on to the numbers 10 through 99 and beyond.

**Warning Sign**
When signing the number three, you might be tempted to hold down your little finger with your thumb while holding up your three middle fingers. Thumbs up, please!

## 10–99 and Counting

This next group of number signs is a little trickier to learn and will require a bit more practice. Stay with us and we'll have you up to a million in no time!

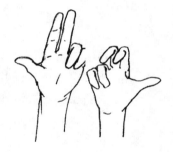

*Ten. Right hand in the "A" position, with the thumb extended up and the palm to the left. Shake your hand back and forth slightly.*

*Eleven. Flick the index finger against the thumb and up, two times.*

*Twelve. Flick the fingers of the "2" hand against the thumb and up, two times.*

*Thirteen. Flick the fingers of the "3" hand down toward the palm and back up, two times. Notice that the thumb stays still.*

The signs for 16 through 19 are interesting. You start each one with a "10" hand, which changes into the second numeral of the number you're signing.

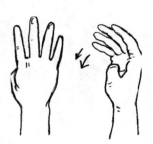

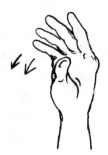

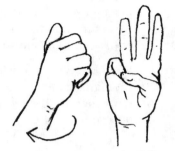

*Fourteen. Flick the fingers of the "4" hand down toward the palm and back up, two times.*

*Fifteen. Flick the fingers of the "5" hand down toward the palm and back up, two times.*

*Sixteen. Right hand starts palm left in the "10" shape, then turns until the palm is out while changing into the "6" shape.*

This repeats for 17, except the handshape changes to "7" while the palm turns, etc. The sequence changes again for the numbers 20 through 29.

With some exceptions, the numbers 31 to 98 follow a pattern of signing.

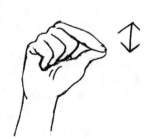

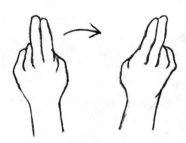

*Twenty. Right hand in the "G" shape, palm facing left, open and close the index finger repeatedly.*

*Twenty-one. Right hand in the "L" shape, palm in. Bend thumb down repeatedly—thumb bends only from the first joint.*

*Twenty-two. Right hand in the "2" shape starts with the palm out, then turns to the right while bouncing slightly.*

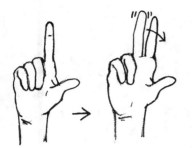

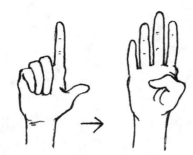

*Twenty-three. Right hand in the "3" shape, palm out. The middle finger bends down repeatedly.*

*Twenty-four. Right hand in the "L" shape, palm out. Bring the thumb in against the palm, as the three fingers that were down come up into the "4" shape.*

*Twenty-five. Right hand palm out. The index and ring fingers bend down toward the palm repeatedly.*

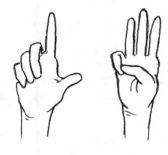

*Twenty-six. Right hand in the "L" shape, palm out. Bring the thumb over against the little finger while raising three middle fingers into the "6" shape.*

*Twenty-seven. Right hand in the "L" shape, palm out. The thumb closes over the ring finger as the three other fingers come up into the "7" shape.*

*Twenty-eight. Right hand in the "L" shape, palm out. The thumb closes onto the middle finger as the three other fingers come up into the "8" shape.*

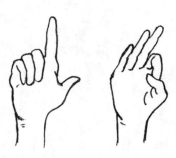

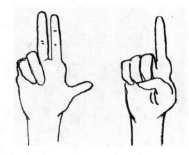

*Twenty-nine. Right hand in the "L" shape, palm out. The thumb and the index finger close together as the three other fingers come up into the "9" shape.*

*Thirty. Right hand in the "3" shape closes into the "flattened O" shape.*

*Thirty-one. The right hand in the "3" shape changes into a "1" shape.*

For 32, the "3" shape hand changes into a "2" shape. For 41, the "4" shape hand changes into the "1" shape. For 56, the "5" shape hand changes into the "6" shape. For 78, the "7" shape hand changes into the "8" shape. You get the picture.

One group of exceptions to this pattern are the following: 33, 44, 55, 66, 77, 88, and 99. We show you how to sign "33," and the other numbers in this group are signed the same way, using the appropriate number signs.

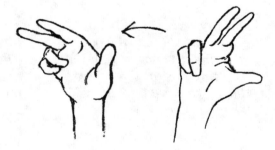

*Thirty-three. To sign 33, the right hand in the "3" shape starts with the palm out, then turns to the right while bouncing slightly, maintaining the "3" hand. The sign shows two "3" shapes, or 33.*

# Oddballs

Some number signs don't follow the patterns that most do. These oddballs, or irregular numbers, fall into two groups. The following numbers are members of the first oddball group: 67, 68, 69, 78, 79, 89.

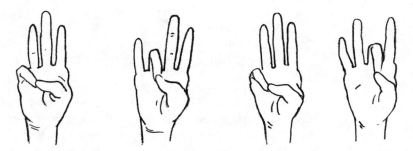

*Sixty-seven and sixty-eight. For 67, the right hand in the "6" shape starts with the palm left, then curves out slightly to the right, ending with the palm out in the "7" shape. Repeat the motion, but end in the "8" shape for 68, etc.*

The second group of oddballs includes the following numbers: 76, 86, 87, 96, 97, and 98.

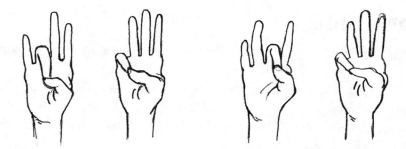

*Seventy-six and eighty-six. For 76, the right hand in the "7" shape starts with the palm out, then bends slightly to the left, ending with the palm to the left in the "6" shape. The motion is the same for the rest of the numbers, but for 86 you'd start with your palm in the "8" shape and end in the "6" shape, etc.*

And, just a few more oddballs:

*One hundred. The right hand in the "1" shape opens into the "C" shape.*

*One thousand. Extend the right index finger up with the palm to the left. Then hit the fingertips of your bent right hand against your open left hand, palm right.*

*One million. Point the right index finger up with the palm to the left. Then hit the fingertips of your bent right hand against your left open palm, then to the left fingers.*

See! We told you we'd have you signing to one million. Now that you've got all that down, let's have a look at signing dollars and cents.

## Dollars and Cents

Because money and numbers always go together, we're going to show you some money-related signs.

**Signposts**

The same movement, with the corresponding handshape, is used to indicate "dollar" with numbers up to 10. Starting with "10," when signing amounts of money, you just sign "dollars" and then the number. If it's in context with your conversation, you don't need to sign "dollars," just the number.

It's interesting to note how amounts of money are signed in ASL. Instead of saying "nine dollars and thirty-five cents," as we would in English, you'll sign, "dollars nine, cents thirty-five."

Although it sounds peculiar at first, think about this for a minute. ASL is a very visual language. It makes sense to see the sign for dollars and cents before the sign for the numbers, because you know exactly what's being discussed. Dollars. Cents.

In written English, we really confuse the issue. We write $9, with the dollar sign before the number. For cents, however, we write 35 cents or use the *cents* mark behind the number. ASL is consistent in its signs concerning money.

Money. With your right hand in the flattened "O" shape, tap the back of the fingers on the upturned palm of your left hand, two times.

Dollar. Hold your left fingers firmly with your right hand, then slide the right hand across and out.

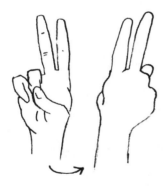

Two dollars. Start with the "2" shape in front of your right shoulder, palm facing forward. Turn your wrist so your palm is facing your body while maintaining the "2" handshape.

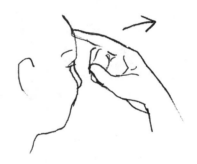

Cents. Bring your right index finger out several inches from your right temple.

# Addresses and Phone Numbers

**Signposts**
Cents is signed the same way for other numbers. Make sure you use the handshape that corresponds to the amount you're signing.

What do you do if someone asks you for your address? Or your phone number? Addresses are signed in a way that's similar to what we'd say in English.

If your address is 892 Miller Street, for instance, you would sign "8," then "92," rather than "8," "9," "2." To give your phone number, just sign the numbers as you would speak them. For example, if your phone number is 222-1111, you would sign "2-2-2 (pause) 1-1-1-1."

# Fractions

Just when you thought you were done with all these numbers, we're going to throw a few fractions your way. Don't worry. This won't be an advanced math course, we just want to make you aware.

*One-half. With your palm toward your body and your right hand in the "1" shape, bring your hand downward from shoulder level while changing it to the "2" handshape. The same applies for one-third, one-fourth, etc. Start with the "1" handshape and change to "3," "4," or whatever.*

For "³/₄," "⁶/₈," or whatever, start with the handshape for the top number and change into the shape for the second number while moving your hand forward.

# The Least You Need to Know

➤ Number handshapes and signs are very important in ASL because they're so frequently used.

➤ The handshapes for one through nine not only represent numerals, but are used as handshapes in a variety of signs.

➤ Learning to count from 10 to a million sounds like a daunting task, but once you learn the patterns of the signs, it's not as hard as you might think.

➤ Some numbers are oddballs and don't fall within the patterns.

➤ Signing dollars and cents makes perfect sense.

➤ Addresses are signed much like they're spoken in English.

➤ Signing fractions is a clever way of expressing how they're written.

# Part 3
# Signs You'll Need to Know

Okay, now we're ready to start learning and practicing American Sign Language. We might as well start off with the signs you'll use most often—those that deal with family, friends, home, work, school, food, and so forth.

Just keep in mind that there are many variations on signs, depending on where they originated, who is signing them, and so on. There are as many as 50 different ways to perform some signs.

You might sign something to another signer who does the same sign much differently. Just be creative and you'll manage to communicate just fine.

# The Family Circle and Beyond

Ah, the family…. A closely knit, happy group of smiling parents, well-behaved children, doting grandparents, aunts, uncles, and cousins enjoying each other's company as they calmly discuss whether the sack race or the scavenger hunt should be next on the agenda. The sun is shining brightly, the hamburgers are cooking to perfection, and everyone agrees it is the best family reunion ever.

Yeah, right! If this doesn't sound exactly like a page from *your* family scrapbook, don't worry. You're not alone. We all know that family relationships can be complex, irritating, and worrisome.

They often become even more complicated when a Deaf person is involved. We touched on family issues earlier when we talked about parents who deny their child's deafness or try to make the child adhere to their values and culture. As you can imagine, these acts can cause a child to feel great resentment toward his parents. Some Deaf people turn away from their families as their involvement in Deaf culture increases. We'll look at these and other issues in this chapter as well as learn some signs for family, friends, and neighbors.

# It's a Family Affair

Think about how you would have felt as a child if your parents had refused to talk to you. They'd take care of you—feed you, clothe you, and give you a bed to sleep in—but they wouldn't talk to you. It was just too much of a bother for them. There is great sorrow and resentment among many Deaf people whose parents and other family members did not learn sign language in order to communicate more effectively with them.

> ## Sign of the Times
>
> Jim Schneck recalls the first time he took his son, Peter, to the residential school for Deaf students that Peter would be attending. Jim and Peter were saying good-bye to each other—using sign language, of course—when Jim noticed other students staring at them. Peter later told Jim the other students commented on how lucky Peter was to have a dad who knew his son's language and was willing and able to fully communicate with him.

Conversely, things are not always easy for hearing children who grow up in Deaf households. One CODA (an acronym for Child of Deaf Adult) said her childhood and young adulthood were not easy. She perceived that her parents, both of whom were Deaf, favored her Deaf sister over her. Her sister went away to a residential school for Deaf children during the week, and was welcomed home each Friday with a new toy. The CODA was constantly asked to be her parents' interpreter and serve as their ears whenever it was necessary, but received no reward for her work.

A poignant memory of this CODA is being sick at night when she was about 10 years old and calling for her mother. "I would call out for my mommy to come, but she never knew I needed her," the CODA said. "I'd end up getting to the bathroom and cleaning up after myself all alone because my mother didn't know anything was wrong."

**Signposts**
Remember the gender rule? Female signs on the lower half of the face and male signs on the upper half? "Mother" and "Father" are good examples of this rule.

Ask somebody to name the three most important things in his life, and family most likely will be one of them. Most of us can't imagine life without our families, despite the problems that crop up from time to time when dealing with these intricate relationships. For better or worse, the family unit is a vital part in the lives of most people, and family members are vitally important.

# Mom, Dad, Sis, and Bro

Let's have a look at the signs for some of those most important people.

*Mother. With your right hand in the "5" shape, palm facing left, tap your thumb on your chin.*

*Father. With your right hand in the "5" shape, palm left, tap your thumb against your forehead two times.*

*Son. With your right hand in the "B" position, bring it down smoothly from a saluting position on the forehead to the crook of your bent, left arm. Finish with both palms up, as if rocking a baby.*

*Daughter. With your right hand in the "A" shape, make the sign for "girl" by sliding the tip of your thumb down your jawline, almost to your chin. Then, with your right hand in the "B" position, move it down smoothly from the right side of your chin to the crook of your bent, left arm. Finish with both palms up.*

*Grandmother. With your right hand open, palm to the left, touch your right thumb to your chin and move away from your face in two arcs.*

*Grandfather. The same as for "grandmother," but start with your right thumb on your forehead.*

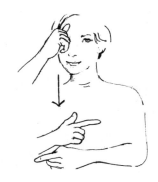

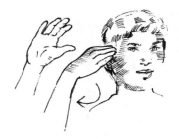

Sister. With your right hand in the "A" shape, move it along your jawline (sign for girl) and down, opening to the "L" handshape and ending up resting on your left hand.

Brother. Start your right hand in the "A" shape over the center of your forehead. Bring it down while changing it to the "L" shape and end up resting it on your left hand.

Cousin. Face the palm of your right hand, in the "C" shape, toward your cheek. Twist your wrist to show your palm, and repeat.

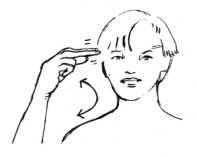

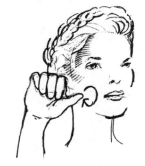

Niece. With your right hand in the "N" shape, index and middle fingers extended and your palm facing your right cheek, twist your wrist outward, two times.

Nephew. With your right hand in the "N" shape index and middle fingers extended and your palm facing your right temple, twist your wrist outward, two times.

Aunt. With your right hand in the "A" shape, palm facing out, make a small, circular shape near your right jaw.

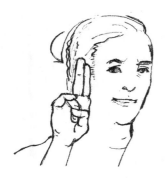

*Uncle. With your right hand in the "U" shape, palm facing out, make a small, circular shape near your temple.*

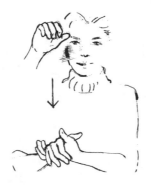

*Husband. With your right hand in the flattened "C" shape, move it down from your forehead and hold it together with your left hand.*

*Wife. With your right hand in the flattened "C" shape, thumb on your chin, move it down and hold it together with your left hand.*

*Baby. Cradle your arms together and rock them back and forth twice, as if rocking a baby.*

*Child. With a flat hand, palm turned down, make short, downward movements as if indicating a child's height.*

*Stepmother, stepfather, etc. With your right hand in the "L" shape, turn it from palm in to palm out on an angled forearm. Then, the right hand in a "5" shape moves up, palm facing left, until the thumb touches the chin.*

## They Call You What?

Names are an interesting part of sign language. As we learned in Chapter 8, it is customary to finger spell a name when making an introduction or first meeting someone. When Sandra and Paul first meet, for instance, they'll finger spell each others' names in greeting.

"Nice to meet you, Sandra," Paul will sign, while finger spelling her name.

"Hi, Paul, nice to meet you." Sandra will reply while finger spelling his name.

If Sandra and Paul like each other and choose to become better acquainted, however, they might give each other shortcut names that can be signed. It is much easier and faster to sign a name than to finger spell it, and names bear special significance among Deaf people.

There are two basic types of name signs: those that are descriptive and those that use a handshape from the manual alphabet. Those that use handshapes are more common than purely descriptive names and can contain information about a person's family or heritage.

Descriptive name signs, which are arguably more fun than the other type, tell you something else about a person. A very thin person, for instance, might have a name sign indicating that characteristic. The same is true for a tall or a very small person. Deaf people typically are not offended by descriptive names, even when they're not particularly flattering. Descriptive names are not limited to family and friends.

Laurent Clerc, the Frenchman we met in Chapter 2 who taught sign language with Thomas Gallaudet at the American School for the Deaf in Hartford, has a descriptive name sign. The "H" handshape strokes the cheek, depicting the scar Clerc bore.

It's a pretty good bet that other teachers also were given descriptive name signs, some of which probably could not be used in this book!

### Sign of the Times

Deaf people use humor and irony in names. Former president Richard M. Nixon has a descriptive name sign which is an unflattering and lasting tribute to his conduct while in office—a modified sign for "liar." Jimmy Carter's name sign is a "C" handshape used with a big, toothy smile. And Ronald Reagan's sign name is an "R" handshape, as in "shooting revolvers," a reference to his days as an actor. We can only imagine the sign names that will go down in history for Bill Clinton.

One thing about names: You usually can't give one to yourself. Forget about giving yourself a name sign indicating "gorgeous hunk of man." It just isn't done. Don't fret, though. There's always the possibility somebody will come up with that name for you.

# Good Buddies and Others

Here are some signs for the people in your neighborhood—the people you meet each day. The signs for people you may meet on a less regular basis—doctor, professor, lawyer, and so on—will be found in the following chapters. Just check the index if you're looking for a particular sign.

*Neighbor. Your right hand starts out pressed to the back of your left hand with the thumb up, then moves out away from the left hand. Add the person marker.*

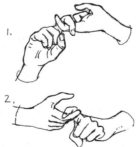

*Friend. With both hands in the modified "X" shape, hook your right hand over your left hand and then reverse.*

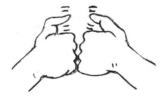

*Sweetheart. With both hands in the "A" shape, put your knuckles together and interlock your little fingers, then wiggle your thumbs toward each other.*

**105**

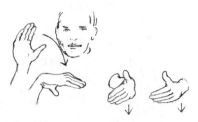

*Man. Put the thumb of your right hand against your forehead, then pull your hand away in the "5" shape. Bring your thumb and index finger together.*

*Woman. With your right hand in the "A" shape with the palm facing left, drag the tip of your thumb down your cheek and along your jawline to an open hand with your thumb on your chest.*

*Stranger. Your right hand in the "C" shape arcs from right to left in front of your face. Add the person marker; this literally means "odd person."*

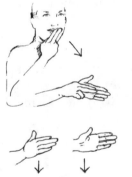

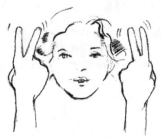

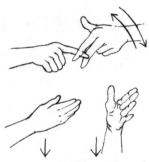

*Letter carrier. With your right index and middle fingers extended, touch your mouth, then move your fingers down to touch your left extended palm. Add the person marker.*

*Barber. With your right hand in the "V" shape, move the index and middle fingers together repeatedly, moving up to your right temple. Add the person marker. This mimics the motion of hair cutting.*

*Mechanic/Plumber. Put the extended index finger of your left hand between the index and middle fingers of your right hand in the "3" shape. Twist your right wrist up and down repeatedly. Add the person marker. This mimics the motion of turning a pipe or a wrench.*

These signs will get you started when you communicate with or about those people who are important to you. They're bound to come in handy at the next family reunion, if you can get somebody's attention between the sack race and the scavenger hunt.

# The Least You Need to Know

➤ The relationships between a Deaf person and the hearing members of his family can be strained due to different values, beliefs, and cultures.

➤ Hearing children of Deaf parents have their own kinds of problems.

➤ Names of people are usually finger spelled when people first meet, but Deaf people often give signed names to family and friends. Many of names are based on how a person looks or acts.

➤ It is usually not considered appropriate for someone to give himself a signed name. Normally, a name is assigned to a person by friends or relatives.

➤ Many signs for people of various occupations are compound signs. The first sign depicts the job the person does and the second sign is the person marker.

➤ You should know the signs now for nearly everyone in your family.

# Chapter 11

# Home and Other Hangouts

## In This Chapter

➤ Learning how hearing peoples' homes vary from Deaf homes

➤ Signing about homes and the things you find in them

➤ Signing about trips, leisure, and common places

Regardless of whether it's a 20-room spread with a gated drive or a two-room walk-up—it's home. Our homes are very important to us, no matter where they are or what they look like. City, country, or suburb; brick, wood, or stone, our homes really are our castles. They house the people we love, the things we treasure, and the memories we hold dear.

On a little bit larger scale, our neighborhoods and towns are also important to us. When we walk into the grocery store or post office and see people that we recognize, it gives us a sense of belonging—of being part of a group.

We value our communities, with their traditions and histories. It's nice to know that the Memorial Day parade will begin each year at 9 a.m. and finish up at the cemetery at 10 with the same ceremony as in all the years past. It's a secure feeling to know that the pharmacist at the local drug store understands your health history and those of your husband and kids, and that you can always get a good cup of coffee and a pleasant chat in the bagel shop down the road.

On the other hand, sometimes it's nice to get away. Think about your anticipation as you plan a vacation. Where to go? What to take? What time to leave? We love to go, but it's always nice to get back home.

When our daily lives change for whatever reason—sickness, travel, or something else—we find we miss our routines. We miss the things we take for granted in normal times.

This chapter is about home and travel, and the places we go and often take for granted. We'll learn signs for some of the things in our homes that we use every day, some of the places we visit often, and some of the places we go when we travel.

## Our Home Is Our Castle

Ideally, our homes are pleasant, happy places where we can relax and be ourselves—places where we can just hang out. The homes of Deaf people, of course, are much like any other homes. There are, however, some interesting differences. Audible doorbells, telephones, and baby monitors are often replaced with visual ones. Flashing lights alert Deaf people when someone is at their door, when their telephone is ringing, or when the baby is crying. Lights can also be installed to alert Deaf people to other situations that normally entail hearing, such as alarm clocks or the dryer buzzer. Many Deaf people use watches that vibrate instead of beeping when set for a certain time.

*Home. Hold the fingers and thumb of your right hand together and then touch below your lower lip, then on your upper cheekbone. This sign indicates the place where you eat and sleep.*

*House. With both hands in the "B" shape, start at face level, then move your hands downward and out at an angle, then straight down. Your hands should make the shape of a house.*

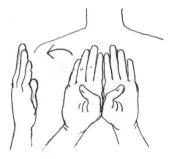

*Door. Put both hands side by side, held in the "B" shape with the palms out. Using a hinged motion, swing the right hand back two times, as if opening and closing a door.*

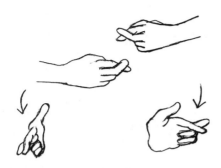

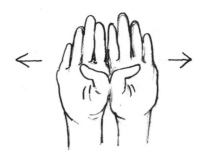

*Room. Put both hands in front of your body with the palms facing inward, held in the "R" handshape and several inches apart. Move your hands apart and to the sides, with the palms facing each other. It's an initialized sign, with your hands forming the walls of the room.*

*Wall. With both hands in the "B" handshape, place them side by side with the palms facing out. Move your hands outward in different directions to indicate the flat surface of a wall.*

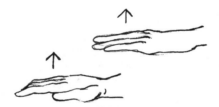

*Floor. With both hands in the "B" handshape, place them side by side with the palms facing down. Move your hands outward in different directions to indicate the flat surface of the floor.*

*Stairs. With both hands in the "B" shape, palms down, move them upward in alternating movements to indicate climbing stairs.*

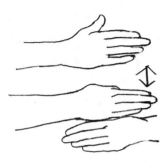

Window. With both hands in the "B" handshape, put your right hand above the left, with both palms facing your body. Tap the lower edge of your right hand on top of your left, as if opening and closing a window.

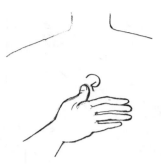

Living room. With your right hand in the "5" shape, palm to the left, put your thumb on your chest and move in a small, circular motion. Then put your right and left hands, both in the "R" position, in front of your body and several inches apart. Move your hands apart and to the sides with palms facing each other. The signs indicate "polite" and "room."

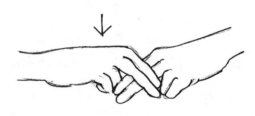

Chair. With both hands in the "U" shape and palms down, curve your right fingers over your flat, left fingers and tap two times. This is also the sign for "sit," but you tap only once to indicate the verb.

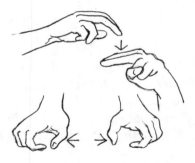

Sofa. Make the sign for "chair," and then, with your hands in the "C" shape and palms down, put your hands together at your waist and extend them out to the sides (indicating the length of a sofa).

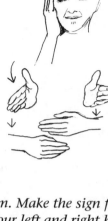

Kitchen. With your right hand in the "K" shape, hold it palm down on your upturned left hand. Flip your right hand palm down to palm up, two times, ending with your palm up.

Bedroom. Make the sign for bed, then place your left and right hands, both in the "R" shape, in front of your body with the palms facing inward. Move your hands to the side, with the palms facing each other. This is a compound sign, using the signs for "bed" and "room."

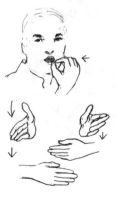

Bed. Place the open palm of your right hand against the side of your face and lean your head into your hand. This mimics laying your head on a pillow.

Dining room. Touch your lips with the fingertips and thumb of your right hand. Then make the sign for room (see the earlier figure). This is a compound sign combining signs for "eat" and "room."

**113**

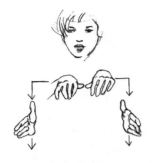

*Table. With both hands open and held in front of your chest, move your hands apart and then down, indicating the shape of a table.*

*Bathroom, toilet. With your right hand in the "T" shape and the palm out, shake it in front of your chest from left to right. This is an initialized sign.*

*Television. Finger spell "T" and "V."*

**A Good Sign**
Remember that sports signs tend to be iconic—that is, they look like what they're depicting.

# A Day at the Beach

Now that we've learned a sampling of signs to describe the home and things in it, let's think about taking a trip. How shall we get there? Airplane? Boat? A train? Or maybe we have some leisure time to fill. What will it be? Golf? Tennis? A bike ride?

*Trip. With your right hand in the bent "V" shape and fingers bent, move your hand in small "waves" from right to left.*

*Airplane. With your right hand in the "I Love You" shape and the palm down, move it up, out and slightly away, two times. This is also the sign for the verb "fly," as in to fly an airplane, but your hand moves out farther and only once when signing the verb.*

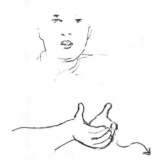

*Boat. Cup your hands with the little fingers pressed together, then move them forward in a wavy motion.*

*Train. With both hands in the "V" shape, rub your right fingers back and forth on the back of your left fingers, indicating train tracks.*

*Bicycle. With both hands in the "S" shape, make the motion of pedaling a bike.*

*Ball. With both hands in the "claw" shape and held in front of your chest, tap your fingertips together a couple of times. Your fingers make the shape of a ball.*

*Game. With both hands in the "A" shape, the palms facing your body and the thumbs up, tap your knuckles together two times. This indicates two teams or people coming together for a game or contest.*

**115**

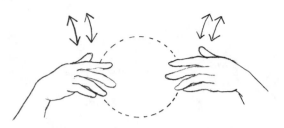

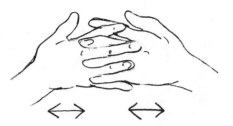

Basketball. With open, curved hands, make a tossing motion with both hands, as if throwing a basketball.

Football. With both hands in the "5" shape and facing each other, move them together and interlace your fingers. Repeat several times. The movement of your fingers indicates the two lines of scrimmage.

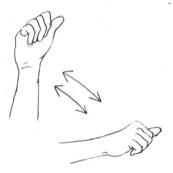

Tennis. With your right hand in the "A" shape and the palm facing left, bring it from your left shoulder across your chest to the right. Repeat the motion from your right shoulder to the left. This movement indicates the swinging movement of a tennis racket.

Baseball. With both hands in the "S" shape, make the motion of holding and swinging a bat, two times.

Golf. With both hands in a modified "X" shape, right hand over the left and palms facing each other, bring them down from above the right shoulder in a large arc to the left. This movement indicates swinging a golf club.

# Places That You Go Each Day

In the course of daily life, there are some places we visit often. These places are usually in our neighborhoods or communities, and they fit into our daily schedules. They're part of our routines. The signs for a few of these places are shown next.

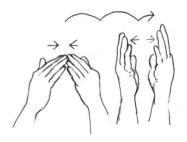

*Store. With both hands in the modified "O" shape at shoulder level, rotate your wrists out twice to indicate ringing bells. (Bells are often over the doors of stores to alert shopkeepers when customers enter.)*

*Library. With your right hand in the "L" shape, move it in a circle to the right.*

*Town. With both hands open and the palms angled and facing each other, bring your fingertips together repeatedly while moving your hands to the right each time. Your hands indicate the roofs of many buildings.*

There are, of course, hundreds of other signs to indicate rooms and objects in the home, leisure-related activities, and common places that we visit. Once you begin signing and holding conversations, you'll quickly learn other signs you need to know.

# The Least You Need to Know

➤ Deaf people often use lights instead of auditory signals to alert them to different situations in their homes.

➤ There are signs for nearly everything in and around your home.

➤ Many of the signs for sports are natural, or iconic signs, representing the action of throwing a ball or swinging a golf club. Many other signs, such as stairs and door, also indicate a visual action associated with the object.

➤ There are hundreds of signs related to home, leisure, travel, and your neighborhood.

(you're fired.)

# Chapter 12

# It's Off to Work (or School) We Go

## In This Chapter

➤ Giving up leisure for labor

➤ Signing work-related things

➤ Understanding the importance of education and schools to many Deaf people

➤ Signing school-related things

➤ Learning that Deaf people are taking responsibility for choosing their schools and careers

Sooner or later, we've got to emerge from our homes and do something. As much as we might hate to leave our comfortable living rooms or pleasant yards, there are obligations that await us.

Most of us, unless we're enjoying the pleasures of a well-earned retirement, either work or go to school. You might be in a traditional job situation, where you leave every morning and return at dinner time. But today, many more of us are working in non-traditional job situations. Perhaps you run a business from your home—conducting conference calls in sweatpants and using your coffee breaks for jogs around the neighborhood.

Maybe taking care of a family and house is your job (and that's a big one!), or maybe you share a job with another person, meshing work outside the home with your family responsibilities.

While once Deaf people were pigeonholed into certain jobs thought to be "appropriate," they are moving into increasingly diverse fields and business sectors. And, as more attention is given to deafness and the Deaf community, more opportunities will become available.

Those attending school also find themselves in different circumstances. You might be attending school full time or part time and living at home or in a dormitory or apartment close to campus. Perhaps you're holding down a job *and* attending school—that's full-time work!

Our situations are diverse, but school and work are big factors in the lives of many of us. Let's have a look at the signs for some work- and school-related things.

**Signposts**

Because occupations are so often indicated by compound signs that include the person marker, let's refresh your memory. With both hands flat and palms facing each other, bring your hands down along the sides of your body. When combined with the sign for an occupation, the person marker forms the sign for the person who performs the work.

## Vocations

There are all kinds of jobs. Check out the classified ads sometime and there will probably be jobs advertised that you've never even heard of! We won't get into the obscure positions that require dual degrees in microphysics and taxi driving from the University of Colombo in Sri Lanka, but we'll cover some basic positions. Whenever possible, we'll give you tips to make remembering the signs easier. Some signs, however, don't have an obvious visual connection.

*Job. With both hands in the "S" shape, tap the bottom of your right wrist against the back of your left wrist. This sign can also mean "work."*

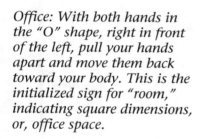

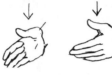

*Office: With both hands in the "O" shape, right in front of the left, pull your hands apart and move them back toward your body. This is the initialized sign for "room," indicating square dimensions, or, office space.*

*Employee. With both hands in the "A" shape and palms down, tap the wrist of your right hand on the back of your left hand. Add the person marker. This is also the sign for "worker."*

*Secretary. With your right hand in the "H" shape, hold it near your ear on the side of your face and move it down to stroke along the palm of your left hand. This indicates a pencil held on the ear, and then writing something on paper.*

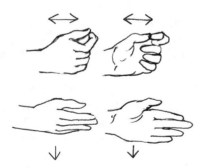

+

*person marker*

*Manager. With both hands in the "X" shape and palms facing toward each other with fingers pointing ahead, alternate moving your hands in and out in front of your chest. This motion indicates holding the reins of a horse (controlling or managing a horse). Add the person marker.*

*Accountant. With your right hand in the "F" shape, move it two times from the heel to the fingers of your left hand, which is open with the palm facing up. Add the person marker.*

121

President. Move both hands (in the "C" shape with palms out) out from your temples to either side while gradually closing the fingers to "S" shapes. This sign can also mean "superintendent."

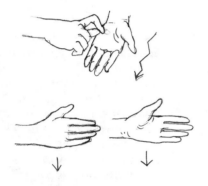

↓        ↓

Writer. Extend your right thumb and index finger together and move across the palm of your left, open hand with your palms facing each other. Add the person marker. This action mimics holding a pencil and writing on paper.

+ person marker

Artist. Move the little finger of your right hand in a downward, wavy movement against the palm of your left hand. Add the person marker. This movement indicates drawing lines on paper.

+ person marker

Farmer. With your right hand in the "5" shape and your palm to the left, run your thumb from the right side of your chin to the left side. Add the person marker. This movement indicates wiping sweat from a beard.

*person marker*

*Engineer. With both hands in "Y" shapes, with palms out and thumbs toward each other, shake your hands and move them in, toward each other. Add the person marker.*

*Boss. With your right hand in the "claw" shape, tap the top of your right shoulder a few times with your fingertips. This indicates the location of military insignia on an officer's uniform. It also means "captain," "chief," "officer," or "chairman."*

## Things You Do and Use at Work

Once you're at work, you need to find something to do until it's time to go home. Attend a meeting or two, talk on the phone, try to figure out why your computer crashed, and so forth. There are people to see and appointments to keep.

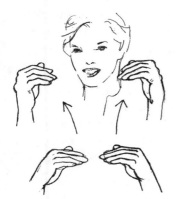

*Promotion. With both hands in the bent, closed "5" shape, move them from shoulder height to head height, indicating "moving up."*

*Appointment. With your right hand in the "claw" shape, circle it clockwise over the top of your left hand. Then close it to an "S" shape and rest it on the back of your left hand.*

*Computer. With your right hand in the "C" shape, rest it on the back of your palm-down left hand and then move it from right to left.*

**123**

*Phone. With your right hand in the "Y" shape, hold your thumb near your ear and your little finger near your chin. This position indicates holding a telephone.*

*Meeting. Start with both hands in open "4" shapes with palms facing each other, held slightly apart in front of your upper chest. Move your hands together to indicate a "meeting."*

*Machine. With both hands in curved "5" shapes, thumbs up and palms toward your body, loosely mesh your fingers and bend your wrists up and down. This movement indicates gears moving in machinery.*

**Signpaths**

The origin of the sign for "school," illustrated in this section, is an interesting one. Typically, some of the boys and girls in schools for Deaf children would have some, very limited hearing. Teachers would get the attention of those students by clapping their hands loudly. The students who had no hearing would see the other children coming to attention and follow their lead. The motion of the sign indicates the teacher clapping for attention.

# The Great Halls of Learning

As you might imagine, schools are of great importance to Deaf people. While many hearing people take education for granted, there are many decisions Deaf people or the parents of a Deaf child must make regarding schools and educational philosophies.

We've included the signs for different kinds of schools that Deaf people might attend. An oral school, for instance, emphasizes speech, and a residential school is a boarding school. Deaf people sometimes call public schools *hearing schools*—that is, a school where hearing people go.

Of course, many Deaf people also attend *hearing schools*, where they encounter different educational philosophies. Education has been a long and volatile issue for Deaf people, who are finally speaking out about what they want—and being heard.

### Sign of the Times

While all children are different, many Deaf children are wildly enthusiastic about attending residential schools. It is in these schools that they can become immersed in Deaf culture and be with kids who share their values, frustrations, and experiences. It is in these schools that ASL was kept alive and growing when it was widely outlawed.

*School. Clap your right hand on your left palm, two times.*

*Class. With both hands in "C" shapes and palms facing each other, rotate your hands outward in a circle. This is an initialized sign.*

*Teacher. With both hands in the modified "O" shape, move them out from your temples. Add the person marker.*

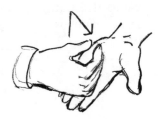

+ person marker

*Student. Start with the fingers of your open right hand on your left upturned palm. Move your right hand upward to your forehead, closing your fingertips to your thumb as you do so. Add the person marker. This is also the sign for "learner."*

*Principal. With your right hand in the "P" shape, circle your middle finger clockwise over the top of your left hand. End by touching the top of your left hand with your middle finger. This is an initialized sign for "over," indicating the position of principal is over other positions.*

*Lesson. With your right hand in a bent "B" shape, touch the edge of your right hand to the fingertips and then the palm of your left hand, which is in an open palm shape.*

*Word. With your right hand in the "G" shape, tap against the upright index finger of your left "1" hand, two times.*

*Finger spelling. Hold your open right hand at shoulder height with your palm down and wriggle your fingers while moving your hand from side to side.*

*Sign. Extend the index fingers of both hands and then alternate circling your hands toward your body. This is also used as the verb form of "sign."*

*Preschool. With both palms open, curve your left hand around the back of your right hand. Then clap the palms of your hands together, as when making the sign for "school."*

*Elementary school. With your right hand in the "E" shape and palm out, rock it back and forth under the palm of your flat left hand.*

*Kindergarten. With your right hand in the "K" shape and palm out, rock it back and forth under the palm of your flat left hand.*

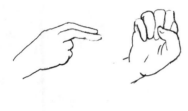

*High school. Finger spell "H" and "S."*

*Oral school. With your right hand in the "O" shape, make a small circle in front of your mouth. Then make the sign for "school."*

*Middle school. With your right hand in a flattened "B" shape, circle it over your left palm, then press the fingers of your right hand onto your left palm. Then make the sign for "school."*

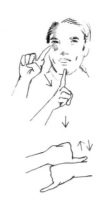

*Mainstream school. With both hands in the "5" shape at your upper chest, move them together and then make the sign for "school."*

*Residential school for the Deaf. Touch your right index finger near your ear, then near your chin (that's the sign for "Deaf"). Then, with both hands in the "I" shape, tap the little finger side of your right hand against the thumb joint of your left hand, two times.*

*Hearing school. Place your right index finger to your lips and make a small outward circle. Then clap your right palm against your left palm, two times.*

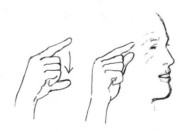

*College. With your right hand flat and facing down, circle it over your upturned left palm while moving your right hand up and down.*

*Gallaudet University. With your right hand in the "G" shape, place it at the side of your right eye and draw back, closing your fingers as they move. This indicates Thomas Gallaudet's eyeglasses.*

*Diploma. With the thumbs and index fingers of both hands forming circles, hold them together to start, then separate them, moving them out to the sides. This indicates the shape of a rolled-up diploma.*

As with Chapter 11 on home and leisure, these are only a few of the signs that are used in communication regarding jobs and schools. Please keep in mind that as Deaf culture becomes increasingly visible and powerful, issues dealing with education and employment will become increasingly important.

## The Least You Need to Know

➤ Deaf people are moving into areas of employment formerly thought *unsuitable*, and enjoying options in work situations.

➤ Issues regarding schools and education may be less clear for Deaf people and the parents of Deaf children than they are for hearing people.

➤ Schools and education are extremely important to many Deaf people.

➤ Many Deaf children and adults embrace the idea of residential schools, where they can become immersed in Deaf culture.

➤ Issues dealing with education and employment for Deaf people will get more attention as Deaf culture becomes increasingly visible.

(Squawk, I say.)

# Pets and Other Beasts

What would our lives be like without animals? Can you imagine your yard without squirrels or rabbits, or your city block without pigeons and sparrows? What would it be like to drive along country roads and see no deer, hawks, or woodchucks? Can you imagine going to a beach with no seagulls, sandpipers, or pelicans, or looking into an ocean and knowing it contained no fish, dolphins, or sea turtles?

And what about your pets? The faithful pup that is *always* glad to see you when you come home, or the cat that curls up against you on a cold day. Whether your favorite animals are the domestic variety or the wild beasts of the forests or sea, most of us would agree that our lives are enriched by the presence of animals.

# Hearing Ear Dogs

Dogs can be particularly important to Deaf people. Certain dogs, called Hearing Ear Dogs, can be trained to respond to sounds such as a doorbell, smoke alarm, telephone, crying baby, or alarm clock, and alert its owner to the sounds.

Such a dog normally makes physical contact with its owner upon hearing a particular sound, and leads the owner to the source of the sound. The dogs are trained to alert their owners in different ways, depending on what noise they have heard. A dog would react differently to the sound of a telephone than it would to the sound of a crying baby.

### Warning Sign

There is a movement on in the Deaf community to save some dogs at risk. The "Save the Dalmatians" movement involves deaf dogs, who are being destroyed by breeders. Their deafness typically results from interbreeding. More information about Deaf Dalmatians can be obtained by writing to Deaf Dog Education Action Fund, P.O. Box 369, Boonville, CA 95415. The e-mail address is DDEAF@aol.com.

Hearing Ear Dogs can be any size or breed, but must be specially trained. They are usually trained as part of a special program at an animal shelter or a non-profit training center. The training period is normally six months, during which time the dogs are trained in basic obedience, specialized skills that employ both hand and voice commands, and *sound keying*, which is identifying and distinguishing particular noises.

Hearing Ear Dogs are matched with people who need them, and the dog and the person who will eventually become its owner spend a week together in intensive training. The dog remains in the Deaf person's home, but ownership is not transferred to the Deaf person until after three months of satisfactory performance by the dog. For more information about Hearing Ear Dogs, contact the American Humane Association at 9725 East Hamden Avenue, Denver, CO 80231.

### Sign of the Times

A Deaf woman who was once left behind in her office during a fire evacuation because nobody thought to tell her the alarm had rung fought for the right to bring her certified Hearing Ear Dog to work with her. She received a lot of resistance from her boss, but finally got permission to bring the dog. Her boss was angry with her and made things miserable to the point where she eventually changed jobs. Her Hearing Ear Dog is welcome at her new job, and she doesn't worry anymore about being left behind or forgotten.

After that period, the Deaf person becomes the owner of the dog, and the dog is certified as a Hearing Ear Dog. The dog's bright orange collar and leash identify it as a Hearing Ear Dog, and entitles the dog and its owner to the same rights as blind person and his guide dog.

These hearing dog programs are supported by donations and community organizations. Consideration is made for people who can't afford the expenses association with acquiring a dog.

# Domestic Animals

Pets are extremely important to many people. Studies have shown that people who live alone enjoy better physical and emotional health if they have a pet. Experts say that kids who grow up with pets learn responsibility and develop a respect for animals. Dogs, cats, hamsters, snakes, or tropical fish—all pets give us something besides ourselves to think about and care for. In exchange, we get companionship and amusement, maybe even loyalty and friendship.

And now, let's have a look at some signs for domestic and farm animals.

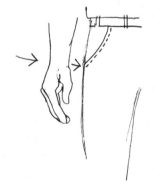

*Animal. Place the fingertips of both hands on your chest, below your shoulders, with your palms facing in opposite directions. While keeping your fingertips still, bring the backs of your hands together until they touch. This indicates the breathing motion of an animal.*

*Dog. With the fingers of your right hand pointing downward, pat your outer right thigh with the palm of your hand. This movement depicts hitting your leg to get a dog's attention.*

*Cat. With both hands in the "F" shape and palms facing each other, move them outward from the corners of your mouth. This depicts a cat's whiskers. The sign also can be made with just one hand.*

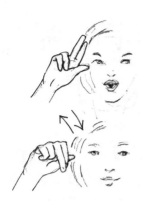

*Horse. With both hands in the "U" shape and thumbs on your temples, palms facing forward, bend the fingers of both hands up and down with a double motion. This depicts a horse's ears. (This can also be done with just one hand.)*

*Cow. With both hands in the "Y" shape and your thumbs on your temples with your little fingers pointed up, bend the wrist forward two or three times. This indicates a cow's horns. (This can also be done with just one hand.)*

*Pig. With your downturned right hand held under your chin, move your fingers up and down several times. This indicates a pig wallowing in mud up to its chin, or having eaten enough to fill itself to its chin.*

## Wild Things

As great as domestic animals are, there's something wondrous about wild things. Have you noticed the increasing number of nature shows on television—the ones that show hyenas stalking zebras, elephants mating, and lions staking out their territory? We're fascinated with animals in the wild.

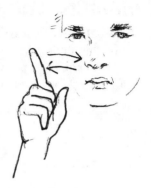

*Bird. This is a fun sign, as many animal signs are. With your right hand in the "G" shape, put it at your mouth with the palm forward. Open and close your thumb and index finger repeatedly, like a bird's beak when it chirps or eats.*

*Squirrel. With both hands in crooked "V" shapes, hold them in front of your chest and move them toward and away from each other about three times. This indicates how a squirrel holds its paws in front of its chest.*

*Mouse. With the index finger of your right hand extended and the palm left, flick your finger across the tip of your nose, two times. This indicates a mouse's twitching nose.*

*Snake. With your right hand in a bent "V" shape, move your fingers forward in a quick, spiral movement. This indicates the motion of a snake.*

*Insect. With your right hand in the "3" shape, put your thumb against your nose and bend the extended index and middle fingers. Repeat the movement several times. This sign also means "bug" or "ant."*

**135**

# Swimmin' Things

Now that we've learned a few signs for land animals, let's turn our attention to aquatic life. Remember when you were a kid and there was nothing more fascinating than a body of water? Creek, pond, swamp—it didn't matter. Any opportunity to get your shoes wet and check out some of those critters under the rocks made for a great day!

*Fish. With both hands in the "B" shape, move the fingertips of your right hand, facing your body, to the inside wrist of your left hand. Then move both hands forward while wiggling your left fingers. This depicts a fish swimming. (This can also be done with just one hand.)*

*Turtle. With your right hand stationary, in the "A" shape with your palm to the left, cup your left hand over the right and wiggle the tip of your right thumb. This looks like the turtle's head withdrawing into its shell.*

# Plants and Flowers

"Mary, Mary, quite contrary, how does your garden grow? " This nursery rhyme is just one of thousands of poems, stories, books, and so forth dedicated to plants, flowers, and growing things. Trees, gardens, and flowers have been immortalized in the stories, paintings, and songs of many, many artists, writers, and musicians. Plants and flowers are not only aesthetically pleasing and give us a sense of connection with the earth and nature, they are vitally necessary to our survival.

Let's look at a few signs for these kinds of growing things.

*Garden. With your left hand held palm down and in front of your body, little finger pointing outward, move your right hand (in the "G" shape) in a circle over your left hand. This is an initialized sign.*

  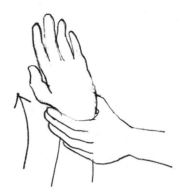

*Tree. With your right arm parallel to the ground, hold your right fingers to your left elbow. With your left hand in the open "5" shape and held up with a bent elbow, twist the palm of your left hand in and out several times. This indicates leaves blowing in the breeze.*

*Flower. With your right hand in a flattened "O" shape, touch your face to the right of, below, and the left of your nose. This indicates smelling flowers.*

*Plant. With your palm up and the fingertips touching your thumb, bring your right hand up through your left hand, which is in the "C" shape with the palm facing right. Change your right hand to the "5" shape as it moves up. This shows the motion of a growing plant.*

Obviously, there are many more signs for animals, insects, and plants than we have space to list here. Hopefully, this will provide a starting point for these types of signs and you'll be interested enough to learn many more.

## The Least You Need to Know

➤ Hearing Ear Dogs serve as *ears* for Deaf people in certain situations.

➤ Animals and plants keep us connected with nature.

➤ Many animal signs are iconic and fun to learn and do.

➤ Many of the signs for growing things, such as plants and tress, indicate movement.

# Chapter 14

# Anybody Hungry?

## In This Chapter

➤ Eating is necessary for everyone, but a pleasure for some

➤ Signing for things about food

➤ Eating in restaurants can be challenging for Deaf people

➤ Learning signs for foods is almost as much fun as eating those foods

It is a rare person who is oblivious to food. Oh sure, every now and then you read about somebody who was too busy to notice he'd eaten nothing but parsnips for the past four years, but I think it's safe to say he's the great exception to the rule.

Some people think about food because they haven't got enough of it. For that, we all need to do what we can, whether with contributions of time, money, or resources.

Other people think about food only when they get hungry. They eat because they have to in order to feel well, but not necessarily because food is exceptionally pleasurable to them.

Other people, though, think about food because they really, really like it. You've known people like this—maybe you're even one of them. *Bon Appetit* and *Gourmet* magazines strewn across the coffee table. The menu for the next dinner party in progress on the kitchen counter. Julia Child is considered one of the family. These people cook because they like to, not because they have to. Meal planning is not a chore, it's a joy. Cleaning up—well, that's something else.

Regardless of your attitudes toward food and all that is associated with it, you've got to admit it's a pretty significant part of most of our lives. Most of us eat at least three times a day, and probably spend a good deal of time thinking about what, when, and with whom we're going to eat.

So, let's have a look at the signs for some foods and things associated with foods and cooking. We think you'll be using them.

## Let's Stay In Tonight

There are some necessary basics when cooking at home:

➤ You've got to have some food. We'll get into the specifics of that a little later.

➤ You've got to have something to cook on, or in (such as an oven or stove).

➤ You've got to have something to eat from, and with, (such as plates and forks). This is not absolutely essential, but immensely helpful.

**Signposts**
The signs for "breakfast," "lunch," and "dinner," illustrated in this section, are good examples of compound signs—two or more signs that are combined to form a separate sign.

Otherwise, there's not a whole lot to it. A little knowledge of cooking methods would be useful, but they say that anyone who can read can cook. Just banter about some phrases like, "I believe I'll add a splash of balsamic vinegar to this spinach before I sauté it with the shallots and sun-dried tomatoes." Whoever you're cooking for will be impressed, and it will sound like you know what you're doing—even if you don't.

Now, say you want to sign about some of the things you'll use when cooking at home. Keep reading and we'll show you how.

Food. With the thumb and fingers of your right hand together, move your hand toward your lips several times with short movements.

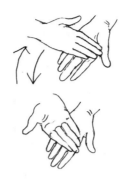

Cook (the verb). Put the palm of your downturned right hand across the upturned palm of your left hand, and flip your right hand over and back, several times. This indicates turning food over to cook both sides.

Oven. With your left hand flat and held in front of you, move your right hand (in an "O" shape) in a circle underneath your left hand.

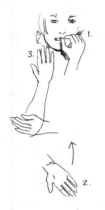

Breakfast. Sign "eat," then sign "morning" by putting your left fingers in the crook of your right arm and moving your right palm toward your face.

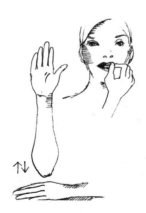

Lunch. Sign "eat," then sign "noon" by putting the elbow of your right arm, with your right hand extended straight up, onto your left hand, which is extended to the right with the palm down. Tap your elbow on your palm.

Dinner. Sign "eat," then sign "night" by tapping the bottom of your right wrist, with your right hand in a bent, open position, on the top of your left wrist. Your left hand is extended to the right.

**141**

*Dessert. With both hands in the "D" shape, tap your fingers together several times.*

*Plate. Use the index fingers and thumbs of both hands to form the "C" shape. With your palms toward your body, indicate the shape of a plate.*

*Bowl. Cup your hands in front of your body with the little fingers touching. Then pull them apart, forming "C"-shape hands. Your hands make the shape of a bowl.*

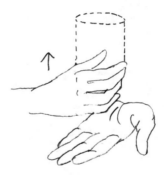

*Cup. With your right hand in the "C" shape and palm left, move your hand down onto your upturned left palm. This indicates the shape of a cup on a saucer.*

*Glass. With your right hand in the "C" shape and palm left, move your hand upward a few inches from your upturned left palm. Your hand indicates the shape and height of a glass.*

*Napkin. Move the fingertips of your flat, open right hand across your lips from right to left. This indicates wiping your mouth with a napkin.*

*Fork. With your right index and middle fingers extended, tap your fingertips against the palm of your open left hand. This indicates the shape of a fork.*

*Spoon. With your right hand in the "U" shape and palm up, make a scooping motion in the palm of your left hand, which is turned upward and slightly curved, then move your right hand upward, toward your mouth. This indicates eating food with a spoon.*

*Knife. With the index finger of your right hand extended out and pointing left, slide it several times down the length of your left, extended index finger. This indicates sharpening a knife.*

These signs will get you started if you're going to cook at home. For those times when you don't feel like slaving over a hot stove, though, let's look at some signs you might need when eating in a restaurant.

## Let's Go Out Tonight

Whether it's the fast food joint down the street or the fancy French place across town, it's nice sometimes to eat in a restaurant. Nothing to prepare and, better still, nothing to clean up. Hopefully, you'll even get some great food.

Deaf people sometimes experience problems in restaurants that extend past figuring out the French words on the menu. Lack of sensitivity on the part of restaurant personnel infuriates Deaf people who say they're ignored, simply because they're Deaf. A server who realizes a customer is Deaf will often ask a hearing member of the group what the Deaf person wants to order. Deaf people are understandably insulted at being treated like a child, or someone incapable of communicating their wishes.

Hopefully, as more people learn about and begin to appreciate Deaf culture, everyone will become more sensitive to these kinds of issues.

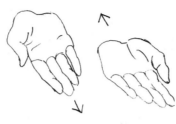

+ person marker

*Restaurant. With your right hand in the "R" shape, touch your fingertips to the right side of your chin, then to the left side, with your palm facing in. This is an initialized sign, formed at your mouth.*

*Waiter/Waitress. Hold both your hands out in front of you at chest height with the palms up. Move them away from your body and back toward your body. Add the person marker. This indicates carrying a tray while serving.*

*Water. With your right hand in the "W" shape, tap it twice to your lower lip.*

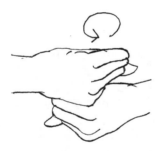

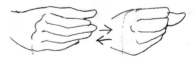

*Coffee. With both hands in the "S" shape and palms toward your body, place your right hand above the left and rub together in small, alternating circles. This indicates the grinding of coffee beans.*

*Tea. With your right hand in the "F" shape and your left hand in the "O" shape, your right hand makes a dipping motion into the left. Or, the right hand can make a stirring motion in the left. This indicates dunking a tea bag in a cup, or stirring in a cup.*

*Milk. With your right hand in the "C" shape and held in front of your body, close it repeatedly into the "S" shape. This indicates milking a cow.*

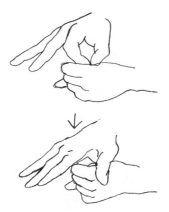

*Soda. Put the index finger and thumb of your right hand (in the "F" shape) into the opening of your left hand in "O" shape. Then slap the palm of your right hand onto the top of your left hand. This indicates the action of putting a cork into a bottle and pushing it down.*

# We're Out of Milk Again!

When you're in the mood to cook at home but the pantry is bare, it's time for a trip to the grocery store. Here are some signs for common foods—the ones you're likely to eat—and run out of often. We've added some non-essentials: cake, pizza, wine, and so on, just for fun.

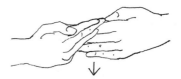

*Eggs. With both hands in the "H" shape, strike your right fingers against the left, then move your hands down and apart, two times. This indicates breaking an egg. To sign the action of cracking an egg, do this movement only one time.*

*Butter. Run the fingers of your right hand (in the "U" shape) over the heel of your upturned left palm, two times. This indicates spreading butter on bread.*

*Bread. Hold your left hand in a bent, open shape with the palm facing your body. With the little-finger side of your right hand, make several slicing motions on your left hand. This indicates slicing a loaf of bread.*

**145**

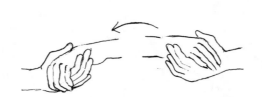

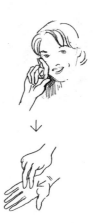

Pizza. With your right hand in a bent "V" shape, move it through the air in the shape of a "Z." Or, finger spell P-I-Z-Z-A.

Hamburger. Put your right hand over your left hand, then your left over your right. This indicates making a hamburger patty.

Chicken. With your right hand in the "G" shape and held near your mouth, open and close your thumb and index finger several times. Then, with your right index and middle fingers, scratch the palm of your left hand. This is a compound sign, combining "bird" and "scratch."

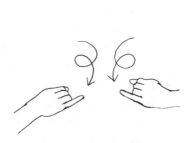

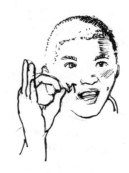

Spaghetti. With both hands in the "I" shape and palms toward your body, start with the "I" fingertips touching each other and then pull your hands apart with a wavy motion. This indicates the shape and size of spaghetti.

Soup. With your right hand in the "H" shape and fingers pointing left, make a circular motion from your left hand, held slightly curved with the palm up in front of your chest, toward your mouth. This indicates eating soup from a bowl you're holding in your hand.

Fruit. With the tip of the index finger and thumb of your right hand (in the "F" shape) held on your right cheek, twist forward several times. This is an initialized sign.

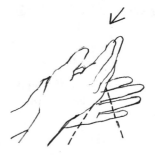

*Vegetable. With your right hand in the "V" shape and your palm facing out, hold your hand near your mouth and twist it slightly.*

*Potato. With your right hand in a bent "V" shape, tap the top of your left hand, held palm down. This indicates sticking a potato with a fork to see if it's cooked.*

*Pie. With your left hand in front of you and the palm facing up, move the little finger side of your right hand toward you twice. This indicates the motion of slicing a pie.*

*Cookie. With your right hand in the "claw" shape, touch your fingertips to your upturned left palm. Twist both hands in opposite directions, two times. This indicates cutting cookies with a cookie cutter.*

*Wine. With your right hand in the "W" shape, put your index finger against your right cheek and move in it small circles against your cheek. This is an initialized sign.*

*Beer. With your right hand in the "B" shape, stroke the side of your index fingers down your lower cheek and repeat several times. This is an initialized sign.*

As you can imagine, there are thousands of signs for food and things related to food. Space allows us to list only a small number of them in this book. We hope you'll enjoy yourself, though, as you continue to learn more and more signs for food.

# The Least You Need to Know

➤ Food is a necessity for all people, but a passion for some.

➤ Many signs for foods and cooking are iconic or initialized.

➤ Deaf people who eat in restaurants do not like to be ignored or talked about as if they're not there.

➤ Food is as big a part of Deaf culture as it is in mainstream culture. As you sign with Deaf people, you'll no doubt quickly learn many more food signs than are listed in this chapter.

# Chapter 15

# Clothing Basics

## In This Chapter

➤ Clothing—born of necessity, evolved into fashion

➤ Signing basic articles of clothing

➤ Signing for things that keep us warm

➤ Signing for things not often talked about

➤ Signing for jewelry and other extras

Ever since early man (and woman) donned animal skins to ward off the winter chill, clothing has been an important part of most cultures. At first, it was strictly utilitarian. Before long, though, people began decorating the animal skins and jazzing them up a bit. From then on, clothing became closely intertwined with the phenomenon we call fashion.

Webster defines fashion as "the prevailing mode or customary style in dress, speech, conduct, or other things subject to change; especially, the mode or style favored by the dominant circles of society."

Applicable to dress, the dominant circles of our society include movie stars and super models, politicians, athletes, and others in the limelight.

Even ancient cultures recognized a form of fashion, dressing in elaborate costumes, complete with headdresses and jewelry. People's dress was an indicator of both their class and wealth, much as it is today.

Fashion has grown into a multi-billion-dollar industry, fueled by our obsession to look good. Consider that women used to lace themselves into corsets, which constricted the waist to nearly inhuman proportions. While they were considered fashionable until the early 1900s, corsets were, in fact, not only inconvenient and uncomfortable, but dangerous.

Today's fashions allow us more comfort—no corsets, thank goodness—but fashion still dictates the wardrobes of many people.

Consider the run on faux pearls when Barbara Bush was first lady. Can you remember all the women who wore pillbox hats to church in the 1960s, a la Jackie Kennedy? Young girls are clunking about on high heels trying to look like the Spice Girls, while Michael Jordan continues to set the standard for athletic shoes. Magazines are packed with advertising, telling us what to wear, when to wear it, and where to buy it.

# Just the Basics

Basics vary considerably from person to person. Whether your basics are blue jeans and tee shirts or custom-made Brioni suits, these are the clothes that you wear most often and are most comfortable wearing. Although our dress has become more casual than it used to be, there are still vocations and occasions that call for dressing up.

It just wouldn't do, for instance, for Bill Clinton to show up for a State of the Union address wearing jeans and a golf shirt. Or for Peter Jennings to deliver the world news in a tee shirt and khakis. Can you imagine Barbara Walters conducting one of her famous interviews in a pair of shorts and sneakers?

In this section, we'll show you some signs for basic items of clothing—regardless of what your basics are.

*Clothes. With both hands open and held at about shoulder height, brush them down along your chest a couple of times.*

 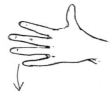

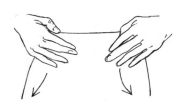

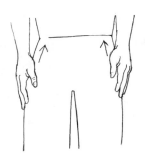

Skirt. With both hands open, brush them down and out from your waist, two times.

Pants. With loose, open hands and palms facing the body, drag your fingertips up your upper legs to your waist. This indicates the place on the body where pants are worn.

Shirt. With both hands in the "F" shape, grasp your clothing just below your collarbone and pull it way from your body, two times. (This sign can be made with one or both hands.)

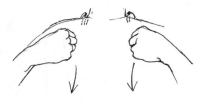

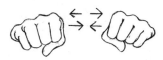

Sweater. With your hands in "S" shapes, palms facing your body and elbows out, touch your hands to your chest and then to your waist. This indicates the motion of pulling on a sweater.

Shoes. With both hands in "S" shape and held in front of your waist with palms down, tap the thumb sides of your hands together. This indicates clicking your heels together.

Socks. With your index fingers extended and next to each other, palms down and hands at waist level, rub your index fingers back and forward several times with an alternating movement. This indicates the motion of knitting needles making socks.

# Outerwear

Now we'll talk about some articles of clothing that cover us up and keep us warm—sort of like the animal skins of old.

*Coat. With both hands in the "A" shape, palms toward your body, bring your hands in an arc shape over your shoulders and down toward your waist. This indicates putting on a coat.*

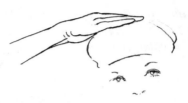

*Hat. With a flat hand, pat the top of your head a couple of times.*

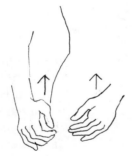

*Boots. With both hands in the "S" shape and palms facing each other, hold them at your left hip and jerk them upward. Repeat the motion at your right hip. This indicates the motion of pulling on boots.*

*Gloves. Use your right hand to stroke slowly down the back of your left hand, held out in the "5" shape. This indicates pulling a glove onto your hand.*

# Unmentionables

You might not spend much time discussing underwear in sign language, unless perhaps you're out to buy some. But still, unmentionables are necessary items, so a few signs are appropriate.

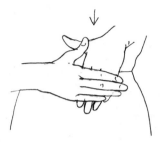

*Underwear. With your left hand held across your waist, fingers closed, tuck your right hand inside the left, as if indicating underwear underneath clothing.*

*Pajamas. Finger spell "P," then "J."*

# Accessories

Once you're all dressed and about ready to go, maybe you'll want to think about some accessories. Jewelry has long been prized in many cultures, and is often used as a symbol of status. Now, you'll be able to sign about it.

*rRing. With your right hand in the "G" shape, move your right index finger and thumb up and down your left ring finger. This indicates the sliding of a ring on and off your finger.*

*Pin. With your right hand in the "F" handshape, touch your fingertips to your chest and brush down once or twice with a short motion. This indicates the motion of putting on a stickpin, such as one used to secure a boutonniere.*

**Sign of the Times**

The sign for "pin" is similar to the sign for the Pennsylvania city of Pittsburgh. The reason is that Pittsburgh was an important steelmaking town, and pins (the kind used in sewing), were made from steel.

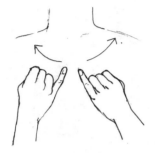

*Necklace. With both index fingers, trace the shape of a necklace on your chest.*

*Watch. With the curved index finger of your right hand, tap the back of your left wrist several times. This indicates the ticking of a watch.*

*Belt. Hold your left hand on your belt line and clasp your right hand over the left. This indicates buckling a belt buckle.*

There's an interesting exercise you can do while shopping for some of the clothing you've just learned to sign. It's guaranteed to raise your consciousness about what it's like to be Deaf. Get a friend to go with you into a store, and pretend that you can't hear. Sign to your friend as you browse through the racks of clothing, but pay attention to the reactions of the people working in the store.

People who have done this report that salespeople often are uncomfortable around a "Deaf" person because they're not sure what to do. Some will ignore "Deaf" shoppers, talking instead to the hearing friend when necessary. Others will go out of their way to be helpful, pointing with exaggerated motions. No matter what happens, you'll get a first-hand view of the difficulties Deaf and hearing people often have while trying to communicate.

## The Least You Need to Know

➤ Clothing has been closely interwoven with fashion from early times.

➤ Many signs for clothing indicate the motion of putting on the clothing or the area that will be covered by the clothing.

➤ Some words, like "pin" and "Pittsburgh," have signs that are similar. There are often interesting reasons for such similarities.

# Chapter 16

# Clubs, Celebrations, and Occasions

## In This Chapter

➤ Joining Deaf clubs and their role in Deaf culture

➤ Getting ready to party

➤ Signing birthdays, weddings, and holidays

➤ Using the signs for etiquette and related signs

Hang up the streamers, blow up the balloons, and bake the cake. There's going to be a party. Most of us enjoy parties and socializing with friends and family. It's a chance to catch up on the latest news and share what has been going on in our lives. For many people, there's nothing better than being with friends, enjoying their company, and having a good time.

# Deaf Clubs

Socialization is just as important to Deaf people as it is to those who hear, and for this reason Deaf clubs were established throughout the country. In 1980, there were 175 Deaf clubs listed in the United States, serving various segments of the Deaf community. Most major cities have at least one Deaf club.

There are Deaf clubs for senior citizens, athletes, African-Americans, Catholics, sportsmen and sportswomen, Democrats, and for other sectors of the Deaf population.

Deaf clubs are not only places where Deaf people can socialize and have a good time, they have traditionally been places where Deaf people can exchange important information and tips for getting along in the hearing world. Deaf culture, values, and customs are passed along from older members to younger ones. Deaf history is shared, jokes are exchanged, and values are reinforced.

**Signposts**

Many Deaf clubs have traditionally been located on the second floor of the buildings in which they're housed. They're accessed by a flight of stairs leading up to the club. The steps are meant to emphasize the club's status as *a place apart*. They are a retreat from the struggles Deaf people encounter in the hearing world.

At a Deaf club, one can find out names of doctors or lawyers who have earned the trust of other Deaf people. Information is shared about such things as the quality of different schools, available housing, and current news affecting Deaf people. Often, Deaf clubs will sponsor athletic teams that compete with teams from other clubs under the auspices of the American Athletic Association of the Deaf, Inc.

Deaf clubs, though still found across the country, do not seem to be as important in the Deaf community as they once were, particularly among younger people. The decline is attributed to several factors, including the increased availability of interpreters. Interpreters make events such as theater accessible to Deaf people, and also make information once learned primarily from Deaf clubs easier to obtain.

Also, increasing numbers of hearing people are learning sign language, giving Deaf people more opportunity for interaction and socialization outside of the clubs. And the wide availability of captioned films, which were once shown almost exclusively in Deaf clubs, has greatly increased social opportunities for Deaf people.

Still, Deaf clubs retain their roles as friendly, non-threatening, and welcoming places for Deaf people to socialize and become more fully immersed in Deaf culture. This is not to say, however, that Deaf people meet only in clubs. Parties in each others' homes are common and many other activities are enjoyed as well.

# Birthday Parties

What better excuse is there for a party than to celebrate a birthday? Kids love birthday parties, and they're nearly as popular with adults.

Let's look at a few of the signs associated with birthdays and parties.

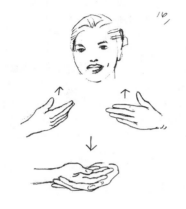

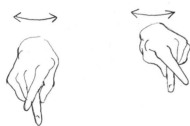

*Happy birthday. Begin with the palm of your right hand held to your chest (the sign for "happy"). Move your hand up and down two times, then bring your right hand down to rest on your left palm. Add the sign for "day" (see Chapter 19). This combines the signs for "happy" and "birth," and "day."*

*Party. With both hands in the "P" shape, swing them back and forth in front of your body.*

*Present. With both hands in the modified "X" shape, move them outward in front of you with the palms facing each other. This indicates handing someone a gift.*

# Weddings

Each wedding is as individual as the bride and groom, but all weddings are special. Regardless if it's in an ornate, decorated church with 500 guests or before a local magistrate with just one attendant, a wedding is an event to be celebrated.

**Signposts**

While the bride has a sign of her own, there is not a widely used sign for "groom." A signer most likely would finger spell G-R-O-O-M when discussing the groom.

Deaf people marry other Deaf people approximately nine times out of ten. In the core circles of Deaf culture, the marriage of a Deaf person to a non-deaf person is frowned upon and discouraged. It is felt that Deaf people should marry within the Deaf minority in order to preserve and perpetuate Deaf culture. Of course, some Deaf do marry hearing people. These couples face some challenges as a result of their differences. For instance, if the Deaf husband or wife is deeply involved in Deaf culture, the hearing partner must recognize that he or she will never be completely accepted. While some hearing people are accepted as part of Deaf culture, they can never be one of the most inner circle.

*Bride. Hold both hands in front of your chest, as if carrying a bouquet.*

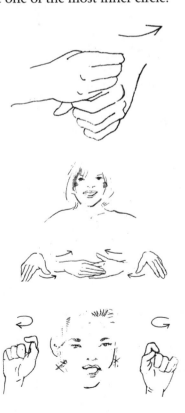

*Wedding. Both hands in a flat, open position start apart, with the palms down. Then the hands sweep together, with the right hand clasping the top of the left. This indicates the joining of the bride and groom.*

*Anniversary. With both hands raised above the shoulders, index fingers resting on the thumbs and the other fingers down, make tight circles in and out.*

# Holidays

There are many regional signs for holidays in ASL. Deaf children in residential schools invented signs for holidays, which spread throughout the Deaf communities surrounding the schools.

We've tried to give you the most commonly used signs for some major holidays, and it's a pretty sure bet you'll be understood if you use these signs. Even so, be aware that regional differences may crop up.

> **Signposts**
> There is not yet a widely used sign for "Kwanzaa," a holiday started in 1966 by Dr. Maulana Karenga to celebrate the culture of Americans of African ancestry. There are some signs for the holiday that are used regionally, one of which probably will spread and become widely used in the not-too-distant future.

*Holiday. With both hands in the "5" shape, double-tap your thumbs to your armpits. This indicates sitting back with your thumbs under your suspenders with nothing to do.*

*Christmas. With your right hand in the "C" shape, palm to the left, sweep your arm across your body to the right in an arcing motion. This indicates the shape of a wreath.*

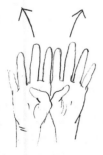

*Hanukkah. With both hands in the "4" handshape, hold your hands in front of you, then move them up. This indicates the candles used in Hanukkah celebrations.*

*Thanksgiving. With both hands in the "O" shape, start them at your mouth and, with both palms facing your body, move both your hands out and then up, opening your fingers as they rise. This indicates thanks, directed toward God.*

*Easter. With both hands in the "E" shapes, twist them in small circles. This is an initialized sign.*

# Thanks, I'd Love to Join You

People are social creatures. Most of us like to be around other people, and go out of our way to arrange and attend social events. These social occasions require a degree of etiquette. There are standards of behavior that extend from the initial greeting to the last good-bye. It just doesn't do, for instance, to barge into a party, unannounced, and proceed to spill punch on the rug without even an apology.

As you learned when you were a child, "please," "thank you," and "Excuse me, please" will serve you well throughout life. So, let's look at a few signs that no doubt will be helpful.

There. You might not be ready to meet the Queen of England, but these few signs should allow you to meet at least the minimum standards of etiquette. Remember that signs that express feeling, such as *sorry* or *thank you* are very dependent on facial expression.

An interesting aspect of Deaf culture is evidenced in parting. Departures occur in stages, and often take as long as an hour. Good-byes are first said in one room, then said all over again as you move to a different room. Good-byes often include plans to get together again and other upcoming events. One explanation for this custom is that Deaf people, until recently, were unable to communicate by telephone. Personal meetings were meaningful and valuable to the Deaf, who rely on one another for support and solidarity. As a result, Deaf friends would linger, reluctant for the time together to end.

*Hello. Start with the index finger of your right "B" hand at your right temple, palm forward and fingers pointed up. Bring your hand out to the right in a crisp movement.*

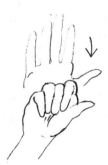

*Good-bye. Bend the fingers of your open right hand, palm facing forward, up and down repeatedly, as in waving good-bye.*

*Welcome. Hold your open right hand with the palm up at your side and raised to about shoulder height. Then sweep down and to the left, ending with your palm up.*

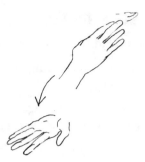

*Please. Rub the palm of your right hand in a circular motion on your chest. This indicates rubbing your heart.*

*Thank you. Your right hand in the "open" shape starts in front of your mouth, then moves down and out, with the palm turning up. You can use two hands to express great thanks.*

*Excuse me. Brush your right fingertips straight out along your open left palm, two times.*

*Sorry. With your right hand in the "A" shape, palm in, move it in a circle on your chest. Repeat several times.*

*Take care. With both hands in the "K" shape, palms facing each other, tap the right hand down on top of the left.*

# The Least You Need to Know

➤ Socialization in Deaf clubs is traditionally an important part of Deaf culture.

➤ Interest in Deaf clubs seems to be dwindling as an increasing number of interpreters and technology such as closed captioning become available.

➤ Most members of Deaf culture favor marriages of Deaf to Deaf, rather than of Deaf to hearing. Deaf/hearing couples may face special challenges within their marriages.

➤ There are many regional signs for holidays, originated by students in residential schools for the Deaf.

➤ Parting normally takes a long time for members of Deaf culture.

# Weather or Not

Did you ever stop to think about how much time and energy we devote to the weather? We spend an inordinate amount of time discussing the weather, monitoring the weather, and preparing for the weather.

We prepare for foul weather—buying coats, boots, and umbrellas. We stock up at the grocery store if we hear reports of a snowstorm heading our way. And then, regardless of whether or not we get any bad weather, we discuss it some more.

We plan our outdoor activities depending on the weather, and NASA officials watch it carefully when a shuttle launch is planned. Some sports events are weather-dependent. Let's face it—weather is a big factor in our lives. It affects our moods and our attitudes, and it can destroy our homes—even take our lives in extreme cases. It is a force with which to be reckoned, and there's not a day that it doesn't affect us in some way.

**Signposts**

A characteristic of ASL is that if a topic has been established, it's not necessary to add an extra descriptive sign. For instance, if you're just beginning to discuss "snow," you'd sign "white" before "snow." This would make it very clear you're discussing snow instead of rain. But if snow has already been established as the topic of your signing, there is no need to sign "white."

Because weather is so pervasive in our lives, let's get busy and learn some of the signs associated with it.

# Climatic Considerations

You no doubt remember from eighth-grade science class the difference between weather and climate. Just in case it's slipped your mind or you were absent that day, here's a quick review. Weather is the day-to-day stuff, the stuff that keeps you guessing. Climate is the long-term consequence of the weather. For instance, if the temperature hits the freezing mark for 355 out of every 365 days in the year, it's safe to say you live in a cold climate.

We can get much more technical if you'd like, but we think eighth-grade science class probably covered it sufficiently. The following signs aren't all strictly climate signs. There are plenty of weather signs thrown in for good measure.

*Weather. With both hands in "W" shapes, and twist your hands in opposite directions several times while pivoting on your thumbs. This movement indicates change, as in changing weather. This is an initialized sign.*

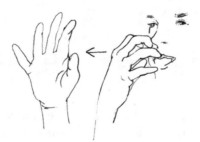

*Hot. With your right hand in a "claw" shape, cover your mouth. Then quickly move your hand away from your mouth. This is as if a blast of hot air hit your hand or you were quickly removing hot food from your mouth.*

*Cold. With both hands in "S" shapes and palms facing each other, shake your hands as you move them back and forth toward each other. This indicates shivering in the cold.*

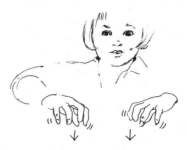

Storm. With both hands in "S" shapes, place one over the other with palms facing each other. Swirl both hands toward the left. The more violent the storm, the more intensity you use in your movements.

Snow. With both hands in "claw" shapes and palms down, start at about shoulder level and move your hands downward, gently wiggling your fingers. This indicates snowflakes falling. This sign is often preceded by the sign for "white, which is illustrated here."

Rain. With both hands in loose "claw" shapes and palms down, move your hands down several times with firm movements. This indicates raindrops falling.

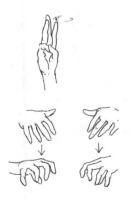

Ice. With both hands in "claw" shapes and palms down, hold your hands in front of your body and squeeze your thumbs and fingers in toward your palms. This indicates frozen and stiff. It's also the sign for "freeze" and "frozen." "Water" is often signed before "ice."

Windy. With both hands in "5" shapes, fingers pointing right and your right palm toward your chest while your left palm faces forward, move your hands across the front of your body.

Sunny. With your right hand in the "C" shape, bring your hand to your right temple two times. This indicates shading your eyes from the sun.

*Cloudy. With both hands held loosely in "5" shapes (right palm turned out and left palm turned in), hold them at about forehead height and circle in and out with your right hand.*

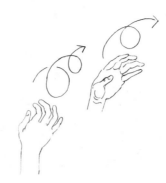

# Natural Phenomena

Rainbows. Thunder. Lightning. These are the special effects of weather. Even in a world of exotic video games, big-screen TVs, and electronic toys, a child will stop in wonder to stare at a rainbow in the sky.

Little kids watch in delight as bad guys are zapped with laser guns or thrown off buildings on their favorite cartoon shows, but give them some old-fashioned thunder and lightning and they'll look for Mom to hide behind until it stops.

As humans find cures for diseases once thought to be incurable, send astronauts into space for exploration and possible habitation, make a cloned sheep named Dolly, and plunge into the brave new world of cyberspace, natural phenomena continues to bring us to our collective knees.

We watch helplessly as homes slide down eroded hillsides, forests are destroyed by fires caused by lightning strikes, and our beaches are washed away. Humankind has not yet found a way to control weather and the phenomena associated with it.

*Lightning. With the index fingers of both hands extended, make jagged, zigzag movements in front of your body. This indicates the shape of lightning.*

*Thunder. Point to your ear with your right index finger to indicate sound. Then, with both hands in "S" shapes, shake them up and down.*

*Tornado. With the index finger of your right hand starting near and pointed down at the upward pointed index finger of your left hand, move your right hand away from the left, spiraling it upward. This indicates the shape of a tornado funnel.*

*Flood. With your right hand in the "W" shape, raise it to your lips (the sign for "water"). Then with both hands in "5" shapes and palms down, raise your hands straight up (the sign for "rise"). "Water" plus "rise" equals "flood."*

*Drought. Move your extended right index finger across your chin from left to right, closing it into the "X" shape. This also means "dry," but "drought" gets more dramatic facial expression.*

*Rainbow. With your right hand in the "4" shape, start it at your left shoulder with your fingers pointing outward and bring your hand upward in a half-circle shape while keeping your palm toward your body. This indicates the shape of a rainbow.*

*Moon. Put the curved index finger and thumb of your right hand up around your right eye, with your fingers pointed inward on your face. This indicates the crescent shape of a new moon.*

*Stars. With both index fingers pointed up and palms pointed away from your body, touch the sides of your index fingers together in an alternating motion as you move your hands upward. This indicates the twinkling of stars.*

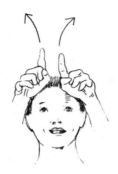

# To Everything There Is a Season

The seasons have been a little confusing in the past few years, thanks to El Niño and other factors that affect our weather. Mountains of snow one winter, followed by hardly any snow the next…Cherry trees blooming a month and a half ahead of schedule…

Still, it has always been, and probably will continue to be, a dependable fact that summer follows spring and winter follows fall.

*Winter. With both hands in "W" shapes and in front of your body, move them sideways, back and forth several times.*

*Spring. With your palm up and the fingertips touching your thumb, bring your right hand up through your left hand, which is in the "C" shape with palm facing right. Change your right hand to the "5" shape as it moves up. This indicates plants growing in the spring. It also means to "grow" or "plant."*

*Summer. Pull the side of the index finger of your right hand across your forehead, changing it into the "X" shape as you reach the right of your forehead. This indicates wiping sweat from your brow.*

*Fall. With your right hand in the "B" shape, brush it down your left arm to near your elbow. This indicates leaves falling from trees.*

Whether you're speaking or signing, conversation about the heat or cold or rain or snow is bound to crop up. These signs will help you get started when you find yourself in a conversation about the weather.

## The Least You Need to Know

➤ Many, many human activities depend on the weather. That makes it a topic that's discussed often.

➤ Extra descriptive signs are sometimes necessary in ASL when a topic is just being established. Once it's established, the extra describers are no longer necessary.

➤ Many weather signs are iconic or natural signs.

➤ One reason people are so intrigued by weather is that they have no control over it.

➤ Some weather-related signs have dual meanings.

# Chapter 18

# Don't Know Much About Geography

**In This Chapter**

➤ Representing Deaf people throughout the world is the task of various agencies

➤ Understanding what's so significant about France

➤ Signing directions and international signs

➤ Signing countries, states, and cities

➤ Using geographical signs

American Sign Language is *the* language of Deaf people and Deaf culture in the United States, but Deaf Americans are by no means isolationists.

Deaf people from different countries have been interacting for many years, borrowing from each others' signed languages and debating methods of education. International meetings of Deaf leaders have been held for decades, Deaf athletes from around the world participate in the World Games for the Deaf, and in 1986 the World Recreation Association of the Deaf was formed to make activities like ski trips, white water rafting and camping more accessible to Deaf people. There also is an important international organization that represents Deaf people around the world.

# World-Wide Organizations

Deaf people throughout the world come together in, and are represented by, the World Federation of the Deaf (WFD), founded in 1951 during an international meeting in Rome.

In 1996 there were about 110 national organizations that were members of the WFD, compared to only 57 organizations in 1980. The General Assembly of the international organization meets every four years in different locations. Each country has two Deaf representatives in the General Assembly, which elects members to the WFD board and sets policies, goals, and programs.

The last meeting of the General Assembly was held in Vienna in 1995, at which time Liisa Kauppinen was elected as the first woman president of the WFD.

The National Association of the Deaf (NAD) represents the United States in the WFD. The U.S. association is one of the oldest national associations for Deaf people in the world. It was formed in 1880 during a meeting in Cincinnati, Ohio, and today has more than 20,000 direct members, as well as associate members through state organizations.

The NAD advocates for Deaf people and publishes books, a newspaper, and a quarterly monograph. It sponsors events such as the Miss Deaf American contest and an annual leadership camp for young people, and maintains a legal defense fund to help in its defense of Deaf rights.

**A Good Sign**

For more information about the World Federation of the Deaf and the National Association of Deaf, contact the NAD office at 814 Thayer Avenue, Silver Spring, MD 20910. The phone number is 301-587-1788 (voice), or 301-587-1789 (TTY).

We can't finish an international discussion without mentioning a particular country—France. France is of particular historical importance to Deaf people throughout the world. It is considered the birthplace of Deaf education for the Western world. The signed languages of many countries (including ASL) stem from French signed language, and Laurent Clerc, the French teacher who worked with Thomas Gallaudet, is somewhat of a hero to many Deaf people.

Now that you've been introduced to the world-wide and national organizations that represent Deaf people, let's have a look at some of the signs that are necessary when considering other countries in the world.

# Which Way to Go?

You can't get someplace if you don't know where you're going. Directions are a vital part of travel, and even of just knowing where you are. Few people set out on a long car trip without some idea of where they're going and how they'll get there. In this section, you'll learn the signs for basic directions so you'll know your place in this big world. These signs are mostly initialized signs and quite easy to learn.

## Sign of the Times

It was a long-held stereotype that Deaf people were not good drivers because they couldn't hear the sounds of the traffic around them. It was very difficult for Deaf drivers to get auto insurance at reasonable rates because of this, and some Deaf people even formed insurance companies to overcome the problem. However, this stereotype is breaking down as studies and statistics indicate the Deaf are safer drivers than many hearing people. The U.S. Department of Transportation released findings saying that nearly all driving decisions are made on the basis of sight, not sound. It's been documented that Deaf drivers have little functional difference than hearing drivers using the heater, air conditioner, or radio.

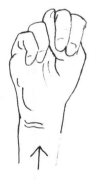

*North. With your right hand in the "N" shape and palm facing out, move it up to slightly above shoulder height. This is an initialized sign, moving "north."*

*South. With your right hand in the "S" shape and palm facing out, move it downward. This is an initialized sign, moving "south."*

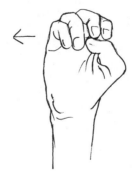

*East. With your right hand in the "E" shape and palm facing out, about shoulder level, move it to the right. This is an initialized sign, moving "east."*

*West. With your left hand in the "W" shape and palm facing out, about shoulder level, move it to the left. This is an initialized sign, moving "west."*

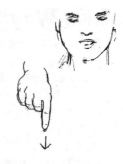

*Right. With your right hand in the "R" shape, move it out to the right with your palm facing out. This is an initialized sign, moving "right."*

*Left. With your right hand in the "L" shape, move it to the left with your palm facing out. This is an initialized sign, moving "left."*

*Up. Point the index finger of your right hand straight up, with your palm out.*

*Down. Point the index finger of your right hand downward, while moving your hand down.*

*Near. Move your right hand (open, with the palm toward your body and the fingers pointed left) away from your body to the palm of your left hand (open, with the palm facing your body and the fingers pointed right). This indicates closeness.*

*Far. With both hands in "A" shapes and palms facing each other, place them together in front of your body, then move your right hand forward. This indicates distance.*

# Where in the World Are You?

There's no question that our world is shrinking. At least, knowledge and interaction with countries all over the world make it *seem* like our world is shrinking. Places that people 100 years ago would never have heard of—much less dreamed of visiting—are now familiar to almost everyone. Some of those places are now important politically, as business and manufacturing centers or vacation spots.

**Signposts**
The signs for "up" and "down" also mean "upstairs" and "downstairs."

Our ability to travel has made the world accessible to many people. A trip that would have taken days or weeks a century ago can now be accomplished in hours.

As we look at ASL signs for some of the countries in this shrinking world, we need to mention international signs. International signs are recognized and used by signers all over the world. The names of countries are some of the best examples of international signs.

Signers from each country have a sign for their homeland that is different from the signs used elsewhere. For instance, somebody from Russia will sign "Russia" differently than somebody the United States or Germany would.

It is becoming more acceptable, however, for everybody to sign "Russia" the way that Russians do. It is considered more culturally and politically correct to use the native sign. You'll see from the ASL signs shown next that many signs for countries are based on stereotypes of the country and/or its people. Although the signs are not intended to be offensive, they sometimes can be. International signs do not rely so heavily on stereotypes and would serve to standardize signs for countries. The transition to international signs is in progress, but it is by no means complete.

*Country. With your right hand in the "Y" shape, rub it on your left elbow with a repeated, circular motion. Your left palm faces your body.*

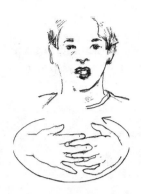

*America. Interlock your fingers and move your hands in a circle from left to right. This indicates the shape of a log cabin.*

*Canada. With your right hand in the "A" shape, grab your clothing at the right side of your chest and pull it out a couple of times. This sign is associated with the Canadian Mounted Police.*

*Mexico. With your right hand in the "M" shape, rub the fingertips down the lower edge of your right cheek. This sign is similar to that for "bandit" or "thief"; this is a prime example of prejudice in ASL.*

*England. Cross your right hand over the back of your left hand, with the fingers of your right hand curled under the left. This indicates a proper Englishman holding his cane.*

*France. With your right hand in the "F" shape and facing your right shoulder, flick your wrist inward, ending with your palm facing out. This indicates a Frenchman flicking his handkerchief.*

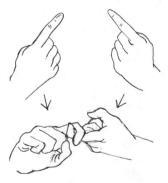

*Spain. With your index fingers extended and curved, start them at either shoulder and bring them toward each other, hooking them together at the center of your chest. This indicates the shape of a Spanish mantilla.*

# States of the Union

There are hundreds of signs for states and cities, and they vary considerably from region to region. Many are initialized, while some indicate qualities particular to a state or city.

Rather than offend our readers by giving the signs for a very limited number of states and cities, we'll leave it to you to learn them on your own if you want to. But, because Washington, D.C., is the capital city and it's an interesting sign, we'll include it, along with the signs for the words "state" and "city."

+ fingerspell
D C

*Washington, D.C. With your right hand in the "W" shape, move it upward in a circular motion from your right shoulder, with your palm facing back. Finger spell "D" and "C." This is an initialized sign made in the position used when signing "boss."*

*State. With your right hand in the "S" shape and palm facing out, touch the top part of your left palm (facing right and fingers pointed up), and then the heel of your left palm.*

*City. Bring your fingertips together repeatedly, with your palms facing each other. Move your hands to the right as you make the motion. This indicates the roofs of many buildings.*

# Is That a Fiord or a Peninsula?

Remember those eighth-grade geography lessons that were full of words like gorge, valley, gulf, bay, and sound? All those terms can be a little confusing, but necessary when learning what's what and where it belongs.

*Mountain. With both hands in the "S" shape, hit the knuckles of your right hand on the back of your downturned hand. Then move both open hands upward in a wavy motion, holding the left hand higher than the right. Use the sign for "rock" and then indicate the shape of a mountain.*

*River. With your right hand in the "W" shape, tap your index finger on your chin, then push both open hands forward in a wavy line with palms facing each other. Use the sign for "water" and then indicate the movement of a river.*

*Forest. Put the elbow of your raised right arm (palm toward your body) on the back of your downturned left hand. Twist your palm in and out a few times and continue to repeat the motion as you move your arms to the right. This indicates many trees.*

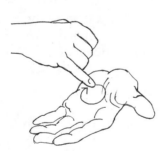

*Island. Use the extended little finger of your right hand to draw a small circle on the back of your downturned left hand. This is an initialized sign that indicates a small area surrounded by water.*

*Sea. With your right hand in the "W" shape, tap the index finger on your chin (the sign for "water"). Then place your left hand behind your right with both palms down and move your hands up and down to indicate waves.*

*Sky. With your open right hand in an open "R" shape, make a sweeping motion from left to right, above eye level. Finish with your palm facing up.*

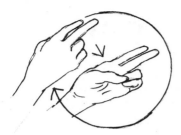

*Universe. Both hands in the "U" shape circle each other. This is an initialized sign indicating the movement of planets.*

*World. With both hands in the "W" shape, move your right hand (palm to the left and fingers forward) in a circle over and around your left hand (palm to the right and fingers forward). This is an initialized sign indicating the shape of a globe.*

Now that you know some signs relating to directions, different countries and geographical terms, you're ready to take on the world. But remember, unless you know international signs, you'll still have trouble communicating with a signer in Belgium or Romania because the signed languages in those and other countries are not the signed language you're learning here.

# The Least You Need to Know

➤ The World Federation of the Deaf represents Deaf people from around the globe.

➤ America's National Association of the Deaf is an active organization that advocates for Deaf Americans.

➤ The signs for directions can be easily learned and remembered.

➤ International signs for countries are becoming more widely used.

➤ American Sign Language is not without some prejudice.

➤ Signs for cities and states often tell something particular about the place.

# Part 4
# More Signs You'll Need to Know

*Now that you've practiced a bit, you're probably getting more comfortable with handshape, palm orientation, and the like. Good! We're going to keep working and learn some more signs that will, undoubtedly, come in handy. In this section, we'll show you the signs for times, days of the week, medical terms and conditions, colors and other descriptive terms, and legal and religious terms.*

*When you finish this part, you'll be ready for jail, church, or most places in between! And you'll be able to ask for the time as well.*

(a little help, please)

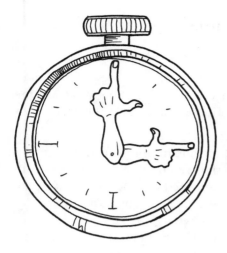

# Time on Your Hands

Time might not seem important if you're sitting on the dock of the bay watching it go by, but to most of us, time is vital. *Time is money. Time wasted is time lost. Time is of the essence. Lost time is never found again.* You get the picture.

It's a rare person, indeed, who doesn't need to be aware of time. Most of us are forced to be rather obsessive about it, for it is a very valuable commodity in this fast-paced society.

**Signposts**

It makes sense to us to indicate future to the front and past to the rear, but don't assume all signed languages do the same thing. For example, users of the Filipino Sign Language do it differently. Any reference to the future is signed to the back, and any past reference to the front. Why? It's a cultural thing. Filipinos say the future is still behind them. It has not yet made itself known. The past, however, has moved on ahead of them and disappeared.

**A Good Sign**

If you're signing the time to someone, usually you'll first sign "time" and then the numbers. If somebody asks you the time, the topic of conversation is already established and you don't have to sign "time" before the numbers.

# Time for ASL

American Sign Language has a means of describing time that is practical as well as eloquent. The body of the signer is used to indicate time. The signer's body is the present, you might say.

Picture an imaginary time line running down the center of the signer's body. The signer's body is the center of the time line. Time that hasn't happened yet, such as "tomorrow" or "later," is signed in front of the body or with forward motions. Time that has passed by, such as "yesterday" or "earlier," is signed or with backward motions, directed to the area behind the body. What could be easier, right?

Indicating the time of day in ASL is also very clever. The left arm of the signer is used as an imaginary horizon, and the right hand is the sun.

When signing "morning," the "sun" will be over the horizon toward the body. For "afternoon," the "sun" will be down the horizon, away from the body. The right hand is straight up for "noon," and "midnight" is signed with the hand down below the "horizon."

# Hours and Minutes

In this section we'll show you the signs for "hour," "minute," and "second." To add numbers to any of these, you simply incorporate the handshape into the sign. For example, signing "minute" with the "3" handshape indicates (you guessed it) three minutes. Signing "hour" with the "2" handshape indicates two hours.

*Time. Tap your right index finger on the back of your left wrist, two times. This indicates where a watch is worn.*

*Clock. Tap your right index finger on the back of your left wrist, then put your hands (both in the "C" shape) at the sides of your face.*

*Hour. With your right index finger extended, move it in a complete circular motion and finish back with your right palm facing your left palm. Your left palm is held up, facing right. The movement of your right hand indicates a complete movement around the face of a clock.*

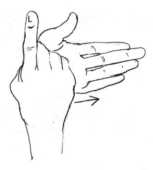

*Minute. With your right hand in the "1" shape and your knuckles resting on your raised left palm, twist your right hand, moving your index finger from the thumb of your left hand across the fingers. This indicates the motion of a minute hand moving around a clock.*

*Second. The same sign as for "minute," but move your right index finger only a tiny bit across your left fingers, with a more rapid movement. This indicates a very small amount of time.*

*Day. With your right hand in the "D" shape, bend your right arm at the elbow and hold it straight up. Put your right elbow on your downturned left hand. Then move your right index finger down toward your left elbow while keeping your right elbow still. This indicates the sun moving across the horizon.*

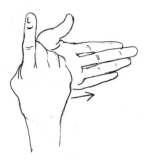

*Week. With your right index finger extended and pointed left, put the heel of your right hand against the heel of your left hand. Move your right index finger across your left palm to the fingertips. This indicates moving across a week of days on a calendar.*

*Month. With your right index finger extended and pointed left, palm facing your body, move it down the length of your left index finger, which is pointed up. Your left palm faces forward. This indicates the passage of time over a month of weeks.*

*Year. With both hands in the "S" shape, start with the right hand resting on the left. Circle your right hand forward and under the left, returning to your starting position. This indicates the earth's movement around the sun.*

## The Days, They Pass So Quickly Now

With the exception of Sunday, all the signs for the days of the week are initialized signs. A "T" handshape is used for "Tuesday," and "T" and "H" handshapes for Thursday. It is common and correct, however, to use only an "H" handshape for "Thursday. The sign for "Sunday" indicates the large doors of a church. If you want to indicate the same day of week, such as, "I go to dinner every Friday," you form the initialized handshape, then move it straight down. This indicates all the Fridays in a row on a calendar.

*Sunday. With both hands in "5" shapes and palms out, circle them out and then in together.*

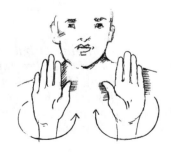

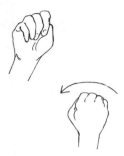

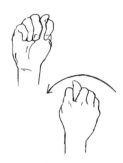

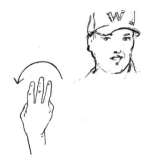

*Monday. With your right hand in the "M" shape, move it in a small circle, clockwise to you.*

*Tuesday. With your right hand in the "T" shape, move it in a small circle, clockwise to you.*

*Wednesday. With your right hand in the "W" shape, move it in a small circle, clockwise to you.*

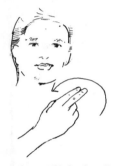

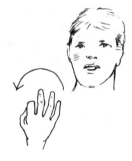

*Thursday. Flick the fingers of your right hand quickly from the "T" shape to the "H" shape, then move your hand in a small circle, clockwise to you.*

*Friday. With your right hand in the "F" shape, move it in a small circle, clockwise to you.*

*Saturday. With your right hand in the "S" shape, move it in a small circle, clockwise to you.*

There you have it, a whole week of days. As you can see, the days of the week are not difficult to learn since all but Sunday are initialized.

Now let's look at some signs that relate to days. Remember how time is indicated in front of and behind the body, as we discussed earlier in this chapter.

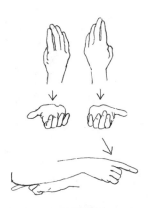

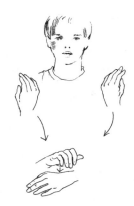

*Today. With both hands in the bent "B" shape and palms in, start below your shoulders and move your hands straight down. Then, with your right forearm angled above your horizontal left arm, right elbow resting on the back of your left hand, bring your right forearm and flat right hand down to your left arm. This is a compound sign that combines the signs for "now" and "day."*

*Tonight. With both hands in the closed "5" shape and palms in, start below your shoulders and move your hands straight down. Then bend your right hand over the back of your left wrist. This combines the signs for "now" and "night."*

*Tomorrow. With your right hand in the "A" shape, move your thumb forward in an arcing motion from the right side of your chin. This indicates movement toward the future.*

*Yesterday. With your right hand in the "A" shape, move your thumb back from the right side of your chin to the center of your cheek. This indicates movement toward the past.*

*Morning. Put the fingers of your open left hand in the crook of your right arm (palm facing down). Move your open right palm toward your face. This indicates the sun moving up over the horizon.*

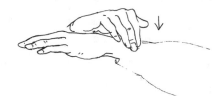

*Afternoon. Rest your right elbow on top of the back of your left downturned hand. With your right hand open and facing down, lower it slightly, two times. This indicates the sun sinking down toward the horizon.*

*Evening. Hit the wrist of your bent right hand (palm down) on the back of your left hand, which is downturned and pointed to the right.*

# From May to December

We'll give you a little break with the months of the year. You won't need to learn any signs for them. Mind you, there are some signed English and Signing Exact English signs for months, but ASL signs for the months are not standardized.

Finger spell the short months: May, June, July—maybe even March and April. For months with long names—that is, the rest of them—just finger spell the first three letters or so, as if you were writing the abbreviation: "D—E—C" for "December," "O—C—T" for October, and so on.

# And the Years Keep on Rolling by

The swift passage of years is brought to our attention constantly with the approach of the new millennium. Before we know it, this century will end and we'll have to get used to a whole new set of numerals.

If you're one of those people who writes the previous year's date on your checks until the middle of February, think of the trouble you'll have (not to mention the trouble our computers will reportedly be having) remembering to write 2000!

You might as well start practicing now. Years are signed the way they're spoken by hearing people. For instance, 1998 is signed "19," "9," "8." So get going on learning to sign "20," "0," "0." Or, you can just sign "2,000." Either way is correct.

# The Least You Need to Know

➤ Time in the future is signed in front of the body, and with forward motion.

➤ Time in the past is signed behind the body, and with backward motion.

➤ Don't assume all signed languages use the same time line.

➤ Numbers can be incorporated with signs such as "hour" or "day" to indicate a specific amount of time.

➤ Sunday is the only day of the week that does not have an initialized sign.

➤ Months of the year are finger spelled because there's no standardized signs.

➤ The years are signed like they're spoken in English.

# In Sickness and in Health

Call the doctor! Call the hospital! What are we saying? First, call the insurance company and make sure it's okay to call the doctor.

Health care keeps getting more and more complicated, it seems. We really need to train our kids to check with us before they fall off the bike and break an arm. Will the insurance cover both the X-rays and the cast? Only a portion of the cast? What about the follow-up visit?

Insurance or none, our bodies keep doing what they do. You feel great for a while, then you notice a scratchy throat. Next thing you know you've got the flu and it's two days in bed. In sickness and in health...

# Body Parts

People come in all shapes, sizes, and colors, but our similarities are greater than our differences. We all have pretty much the same parts, exquisitely designed to work together to keep our bodies functioning.

While we can't list signs for all the body parts (there are about a zillion of them), we can give you signs for some of the major ones.

With the exception of "brain" and "heart" (you're on your own for courage), we won't be getting into signs for internal body parts in this book. You'll have to do some additional research if you want to learn to sign "spleen" or "pancreas."

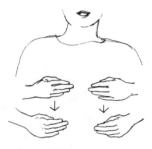

*Body. With both hands open, put your palms on your upper torso, then move them down to your lower torso.*

*Head. With your right hand bent, touch your temple, then your jaw. This indicates the location of the head.*

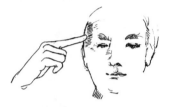

*Brain. Put the index finger of your right hand to your temple. This also means "mind" and "think;" for "think," add a circular movement with your finger.*

*Ears. With your right hand in the "A" shape, grab your right earlobe between your thumb and index finger. This indicates the location of the ear.*

*Eyes. With the index finger of your right hand extended and your palm toward your face, point up at each eye. This indicates the location of the eyes.*

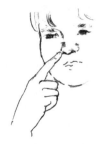

*Nose. With your right index finger extended and the palm facing in, touch your fingertip to the tip of your nose. This indicates the location of the nose.*

Mouth. With your right index finger extended and your palm toward your face, circle your mouth with your fingertip. This indicates location and shape of the mouth.

Back. Reach over your right shoulder with your right hand and tap your fingertips on the back of your shoulder. This indicates the location of the back.

Stomach. With your right hand in a bent "5" shape, tap just above your waist, two times. This indicates the location of the stomach.

Arm. Move the palm of your right hand up and down your left arm, which is slightly bent. This indicates the location and shape of the arm.

Hands. Drag your right palm over the back of your left open hand, with both palms facing your body. Repeat the movement with your left palm over the back of your right hand. This indicates the location of the hands.

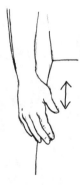

Legs. Tap your right thigh with your right hand, or finger spell "L—E—G."

193

*Feet. With your right index finger extended, point first to your left foot, then to your right. This indicates the location of the feet.*

*Finger. With your right index finger extended, touch your left fingers, one by one. This indicates the location of the fingers.*

*Heart. With your right hand in the "5" shape, touch your middle finger to the center of your chest. This indicates the location of the heart.*

Now that we've learned a few body parts, let's learn some basic signs relating to sickness and health.

# Medical Terms

**A Good Sign**
Kim Horn, technical advisor to this book, teaches basic sign language to emergency medical technicians and police officers. Kim's husband, who is a policeman, says experience has shown him that Deaf people involved in an accident or the victim of a crime are immediately and greatly reassured when someone can sign to them at the scene. Kim says training programs such as these are a sign of increasing sensitivity toward Deaf people.

It's a rare person who enjoys a stay in a hospital. Most of us would not look forward to such a visit, and would want to spend as short a time as possible there.

Although the situation is improving as awareness and sensitivity increase among the medical profession, Deaf patients have traditionally experienced difficulties in hospitals.

Think about being in a hospital. It's a strange place, with lots of sounds. There are near-constant messages delivered over loudspeaker systems. Intercom systems allow nurses to speak to patients in their beds (if the patients can hear them). There are bells and beeps and buzzers. The sounds serve to let patients know something of what's going on in the building. They know Dr. Williams is wanted on line 99, and that there is an emergency in the cardiac unit. A Deaf patient, however, can be extremely isolated.

Most of the medical staff won't know sign language, so they can't communicate very well with a Deaf patient. What happens if the Deaf person is right-handed, but the nurse puts an IV in his right arm? That means the Deaf person can neither sign nor write, rendering him virtually unable to communicate.

What happens if a Deaf patient presses a button to summon a nurse, and the nurse, not realizing the patient is Deaf, asks over the intercom what the patient needs? What if a Deaf person is groggy from a pre-surgery shot and having trouble keeping his eyes open? How will he know that the doctor is explaining the surgery procedure?

There are many things that have in the past made hospital stays frightening and uncomfortable for Deaf people. Fortunately, things are changing. A spokesperson for Reading Hospital and Medical Center, a hospital in West Reading, Pennsylvania, with a staff of 3,300 people, said 70 of those staff members are trained to serve as interpreters for people who don't speak English. Several interpreters are also available at all times for Deaf patients, easing the anxiety of their hospital stays. Many other hospitals across the country have similar programs.

Here are some signs that are related to illness and hospitals. There are many signs for particular illnesses, both physical and mental, but we've only got space to show you a few of them. The sign for "sick" indicates a general, non-specified condition of illness.

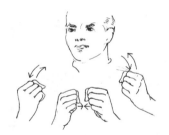

*Hospital. With your right hand in the "H" shape, use your fingertips to draw a small cross on your upper left arm. This is an initialized sign indicating the shape of a cross as found on some medical uniforms, or the Red Cross symbol.*

*Sick. With both hands in bent "5" shapes, touch the middle finger of your right hand to your forehead, while at the same time touching the middle finger of your left hand to your stomach. This indicates pain in the head and body.*

*Accident. With both hands in the curved "5" shape, move them together in front of your body, about shoulder height. Close them into "S" shapes as they bump together in the middle of your chest. This indicates two objects crashing together.*

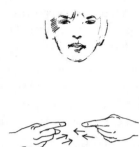
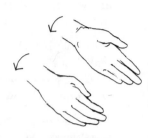

*Medicine. With your right hand in the "5" shape and palm down, rub your bent middle finger on your upturned left palm. This indicates grinding medicine with a mortar and pestle.*

*Operation. With your right hand in the "A" shape, drag the tip of your thumb along the length of your open left hand, held palm up. This indicates an incision; the sign is often done at the part of the body where the incision was made.*

*Pain. Bring the extended index fingers of both hands together several times so that they almost touch each other. This indicates stabbing pain; this sign is often done at the part of the body where pain is felt.*

*Death. Start with the palm of your right hand turned down and your left turned up. Then turn both hands over.*

Well, let's hope you don't need to use that last one very often. Like it or not, though, illness and death are a part of life.

## Medical Conditions

Following are the signs for some common illnesses next. We throw in "pregnant" because it's a medical condition. (Please be assured we don't consider it an illness!) Here's hoping your medical conditions never rate anything more serious than a stomachache.

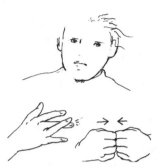

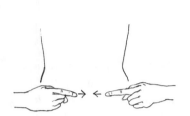

*Stomachache. Make the sign for "pain" as described earlier at the location of your stomach. This indicates pain in the stomach.*

*Pregnant. With your right hand in the "5" shape, move it upward and outward from your lower stomach. This indicates the shape and size of a pregnant woman's stomach.*

*Heart attack. With your right hand in the "5" shape, touch your middle finger to the center of your chest (sign for "heart"). Then, hit your downturned right palm onto the top of your left "S" hand, turned with the palm to the right (sign for "attack").*

# Emotions

Now that we've had a quick course on medical and physical-related signs, let's look briefly at signs relating to our emotions. Medical studies have presented more and more evidence lately on the relationship between our physical and emotional health. Stress, anxiety, fear, and depression wreak havoc with our physical wellness, as well as our emotional states.

On the flip side, laughter, joy, closeness to others, and love have been shown to contribute to our well-being and perhaps even help us live longer.

**A Good Sign**
Remember our discussion on facial expression in Chapter 6? Facial expression is very important with signs that convey emotion.

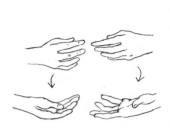

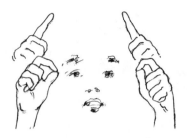

*Tired. Start with the fingertips of both bent hands on your chest, then drop your hands down and lay the little-finger sides of your hands against your chest. This indicates collapsing as if extremely tired.*

*Lonely. With the index finger of your right hand extended and your palm turned to the left, move your hand downward slowly and smoothly. This indicates being silent and alone.*

*Surprised. With both hands in the "S" shape, put them up near your eyes at the sides of your face (palms facing your head), and flick your index fingers up quickly. This indicates the movement of your eyes opening wide in surprise.*

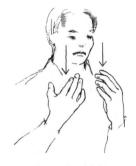

*Angry. With both hands in the "claw" shape with the knuckles pointed toward each other and palms toward your body, bring them up and out from the center of your waist toward your shoulders. This indicates anger rising up through your body.*

*Happy. With your right hand flat and the fingers pointed left, move your hand up along your chest and then outward. This sign is often made with two hands. You should make a happy face with this sign.*

*Sad. With both hands in the "5" shape and your palms facing your body, move your hands down from the sides of your face. You should make a sad face with this sign.*

Well, we hate to end on a sad note, but it's time to move on. Health and illness (especially illness) are topics that people seem to like to discuss, so these signs no doubt will come in very handy someday.

# The Least You Need to Know

➤ Many signs for body parts indicate the location of the part.

➤ Deaf people have faced special challenges as hospital patients.

➤ Sensitivity to the Deaf on the part of medical personnel is increasing.

➤ Many signs indicating emotion require pronounced facial expression.

# Chapter 21

# How Would You Describe That?

**In This Chapter**

➤ Using descriptive words—a dime a dozen

➤ Watch where you put that adjective

➤ Modifying words in ASL

➤ Signing for colors and physical characteristics

➤ Signing for sizes and personal qualities

We use dozens of descriptive words every day. You tell the server at the coffee shop that you want *black* coffee and a *toasted* bagel. You tell your friend at the office that she looks really *pretty* in her *green* dress and you just love her *new blue* shoes. You tell your child to wear the *yellow* jacket and comment on how *tall* the *beautiful* flowers in the garden have grown. We go on and on all day long with descriptive words.

In this chapter we'll take a look at how to sign some of those often-used descriptive words. But first, we'll tell you a little bit about where adjectives are placed when using ASL.

# Where Does the Adjective Go?

Unlike English, but like some other languages such as Spanish, adjectives in ASL generally *follow* the words they are describing. Instead of signing "black dog," for example, you would sign "dog black." It's as though you're saying "the dog that is black."

**Signposts**
The signs for many colors are initialized, but some have interesting origins. The sign for "red," for instance, indicates red lips. The sign for "white" indicates a white shirt, and the sign for "orange" indicates squeezing oranges.

If you're using a noun as an adjective, however, it will come before the word it modifies. "Christmas tree," "basketball hoop," and "party dress" are examples of this rule.

Remember, too, that signs showing size, color, or other descriptive qualities can be incorporated into signs for nouns or adjectives through the use of facial expression, handshape, and the intensity with which a sign is made. It is easy in ASL to distinguish "bad" from "horrible" or "awful."

# It's a Colorful World

Colors are used very often as descriptive words, so we'll begin with those signs.

*Black. With your right index finger extended, pointing left with the palm down, drag it across your forehead from left to right.*

*White. With your right hand in the "5" shape, put your thumb and fingertips on your chest and then move your hand outward while closing your thumb and fingertips.*

*Brown. With your right hand in the "B" shape, move the index finger of that hand down your cheek. Your palm faces outward. This is an initialized sign.*

*Red. With the index finger of your right hand extended, stroke your lip with a downward motion and repeat.*

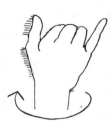

*Green. With your right hand in the "G" shape, hold it in front of your chest and twist your wrist several times. This is an initialized sign.*

*Yellow. With your right hand in the "Y" shape, hold it in front of your chest and twist your wrist several times. This is an initialized sign.*

*Blue. With your right hand in the "B" shape, hold it in front of your chest and twist your wrist several times. This is an initialized sign.*

*Pink. With your right hand in the "P" shape, stroke your lip in a downward motion with your middle finger and repeat. This is similar to red, but initialized to show pink.*

*Purple. With your right hand in the "P" shape, hold it in front of your chest and twist your wrist several times. This is an initialized sign.*

*Orange. With your right hand in the "C" shape, put it in front of your mouth and repeat the motion of closing it to the "S" shape and reopening it to the "C" shape. This sign is used for both the color and the fruit.*

There. Now you can describe a rainbow using ASL. The signs for colors shouldn't be too difficult to remember if you keep in mind that many of them are initialized signs, and almost all repeat the motion of the sign.

# Things That (some) People Are

Most of us spend a good bit of time discussing other people. Inevitably, we look for ways to describe the people we discuss. Here is a sampling of the many signs that can be used to describe a person.

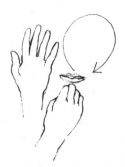

*Pretty. With your right hand in the "5" shape, circle your palm in front of your face. Close your fingertips and thumb together when your hand is at your chin. This indicates a pretty face.*

*Ugly. With your right index finger extended and pointed to the left in front of your face, move your hand to the right while curling your index finger into the "X" handshape.*

*Smart. Start with the index finger of your right hand bent against your forehead, then bring it straight out, away from your head. This indicates wisdom coming from the brain.*

*Deaf. With the index finger of your right hand extended, touch your ear, then make the sign for "closed" by brining both open hands toward each other until your index fingers touch. This indicates ears are closed.*

*Hearing. With the index finger of your right hand in front of your mouth and pointed left, move it outward in a circular motion. This indicates hearing people.*

*Blind. With your right hand in a bent "V" shape, put your hand in front of your eyes and pull it down slightly. This indicates that the eyes are shut.*

Those are just a few of the many signs that can be used to describe a person.

# Size Matters

Size—especially when it pertains to people—is a big issue in our weight-obsessed society. But we use also size to describe other things, and we use it a lot. We order a *large* soda or pizza, or describe the *tiny* baby we saw in church. Perhaps there was a *huge* pile of leaves raked in the yard, or a very *tall* sunflower in the field.

Here are some signs for common adjectives describing size.

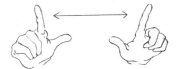

*Large. With both hands in "L" shapes and your palms toward your chest, turn your hands while moving them outward past your shoulders, ending with your palms turned out. This initialized sign indicates a big area.*

*Small. With both hands in "open palm" shapes and your palms facing each other, start with your hands held in front of you at either side of your body. Move your hands together so there is just a little space between them. Repeat the motion. This shows a small area.*

*Tall. Slide the extended index finger of your right hand up the palm of your left hand. The palm of your left hand faces right, with the fingers straight up. This indicates height.*

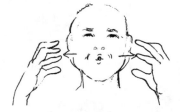

*Short. With your right hand held palm down at your right side, move it downward. This indicates a low height; this sign is similar to that for "child."*

*Thin. With both hands in "I" shapes, start with the right hand above the left, but touching. With both your palms facing your body, move your right hand up and your left hand down.*

*Fat. With both hands in "claw" shapes, hold them up to your cheeks and move them outward, away from your face. Puff out your cheeks while making this sign.*

## Personal Qualities on the Inside

We all know that you can't judge a book by its cover and beauty is only skin deep. Our society places great emphasis on appearance, but when it's all said and done, it's character that counts. Some of the tips we provide to help you remember signs more easily are sorely outdated. For instance, the sign for "polite" indicates ruffles on the front of a gentleman's shirt. There are few gentlemen today who wear ruffled shirts, but the tips do make the signs easier to remember.

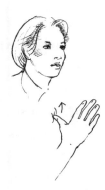

*Polite.* With your right hand in the "5" shape, tap your thumb against the center of your chest, moving it slightly upward. Repeat the motion. This indicates the ruffles found on the shirt of a gentleman.

*Kind.* With both hands in "B" shapes and both palms facing your body, circle your right hand over and around your left. This indicates helping by putting a bandage on someone who is hurt.

*Lazy.* With your right hand in the "L" shape and the thumb pointing up, tap the palm side of your hand on your heart two times. This is an initialized sign.

*Funny.* Move the extended index and middle fingers of your right hand down your nose. Repeat the motion. This indicates your nose twitching when something is funny.

*Friendly.* With both hands in "5" shapes and your palms facing your body at shoulder height, wiggle your fingers and your hands while moving them up. This also means "cheerful," so smile when you make this sign!

*Proud.* With your right hand in the "A" shape, move your downward-pointed thumb from near the middle of your waist up to the top of your chest. This indicates feelings rising within the body.

# The Least You Need to Know

➤ Placement of adjectives is different in ASL than in English—the descriptive adjective comes after the noun.

➤ Facial expression and intensity of signing can also serve as modifiers in ASL.

➤ Many signs for colors are initialized, and most of them are signs with repeated motion.

➤ "Proud" is an important sign as it pertains to Deaf culture.

(Naughty Naughty)

# Chapter 22

# Crime and Punishment

## In This Chapter

➤ Dealing with problems of Deaf people in the legal system

➤ Signing for those who help

➤ Signing for crimes

➤ Signing justice-related signs

If you've ever had to deal extensively with the justice and/or legal system in any capacity, you know how mind-boggling the experience can be. For many people, dealing with police, judges and magistrates, lawyers, and court staff can be intimidating and over-whelming.

The experience can be greatly intensified for Deaf people who are forced to try to make sense out of system they don't understand and with which they can't communicate.

In this chapter, we'll take a look at some special problems Deaf people encounter when dealing with the legal system, as sell as some signs for things related to crime and punish-ment.

# Pull Over!

Imagine being pulled over by a zealous traffic cop who tells you that you were driving 40 miles per hour in a 35-mile-per-hour zone. He tells you he needs to see your driver's license and registration and he wants you to stay in your car while he writes you a ticket. But you can't understand what he's saying because you can't hear him! Talk about intimidating!

**A Good Sign**
Emergency personnel who are able to communicate with a Deaf person in even a limited capacity during an emergency situation see pronounced results. A Deaf person gains comfort and assurance when he knows there is someone on hand with whom he can communicate.

For example, the following is a true story. A Deaf man had too much to drink and was pulled over for drunken driving on his way home. The Deaf man tried to communicate to the policeman who pulled him over that he couldn't hear or understand what the policeman was saying. The Deaf man motioned to the glove compartment of his car, where he had paper and a pencil. The policeman, who said later he thought the Deaf man was reaching for a gun, pulled the man from his car, threw him on the ground, and held his face in the snow with his foot until backup arrived.

Things are improving somewhat, as some police departments are providing basic sign language instruction for their employees. The situation, however, is still a long way from satisfactory.

# Order in the Court

While dealing with police can be intimidating, so can going into a courtroom. Some claim that Deaf people over the years have been routinely denied the right to legal services because of a lack of lawyers with whom they can communicate, or a lack of interpreters to help them.

The situation is not as grim in the United States as in many other countries, but it's still far from perfect. The Americans with Disabilities Act and other U.S. laws state that Deaf people have rights to interpreters in certain circumstances. Trying to find interpreters when those circumstances occur, however, is not always easy. There often just aren't enough interpreters available, and those that are available aren't always competent.

One problem that occurs is that cultural differences make it difficult for Deaf people to get along in the hearing legal system. It is a trait of members of Deaf culture to tell a story from beginning to end, leaving nothing out. Deaf people have a very difficult time answering just "yes" or "no" to questions that they are asked when testifying in a legal proceeding. They want to give additional information, and become frustrated when told not to.

Signers do best when asked one question at a time. Signing, especially when done through an interpreter, does not lend itself to dealing with three or four questions at a time. And yet, lawyers often do just that. They'll ask multiple questions in one sentence, making it confusing for the Deaf person who is supposed to answer. Unfortunately, the Deaf person may appear to be less intelligent than he really is in this sort of situation.

### Sign of the Times

Court interpreters who are fluent in ASL and connected with the Deaf community, sometimes find it difficult to remain neutral during legal proceedings involving a Deaf person. They sometimes feel a deaf person is treated unfairly in court because of difficulty communicating with lawyers and judges.

Hopefully, as Deaf people continue to assert their rights to basic services and other rights, these injustices that have plagued them will be corrected.

Another difficulty occurs when Deaf people have to read and sign contracts, leases, or other documents. Many Deaf people are not good readers because they've never learned the English language very well. And yet, they're embarrassed to admit they can't read well because they don't want to appear unintelligent. So they stumble along, barely able to read a complicated document, much less fully understand its contents.

# Keeping the Peace

If you've ever glanced in your rear-view mirror, only to see a police car with its lights flashing and obviously intended for you, then you know the feelings of dread a cop encounter can generate. If you've ever needed help and a police officer has come to your aid, then you understand the appreciation and respect that good cops earn and deserve. Police, and other emergency personnel such as firefighters and ambulance crews, are very important in our society.

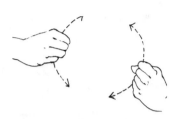

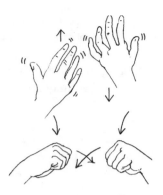

*Police. With your right hand in the "C" shape, put it just below your left shoulder and tap twice. This indicates the shape of a badge.*

*Police car. Make the sign for "police" (see previous illustration), and then the sign for "car" by moving both hands (in "S" shapes and palms toward your body) up and down in alternating movements. The sign for "car" indicates the motion of steering a car.*

*Firefighter. With both hands in "5" shapes, wiggle your fingers and move your hands up and down in alternating movements. Then, with both hands in "S" shapes and palms facing each other, bring your hands across your body, ending with your wrists crossed in front of your chest. This is the sign for "fire" and the sign for "fight."*

## Lock 'Em Up!

Crime isn't a pleasant topic, but it can't be ignored. Here are some crime-related signs.

### Sign of the Times

Deaf advocates say the rights of Deaf people are often violated when they're taken into custody. Police officers who arrest a Deaf person and don't know sign language often use a written Miranda warning if an interpreter is not available. The warning, which informs a person in custody of his rights, is beyond the reading capacity of many Deaf people, but a Deaf person in custody may sign a waiver indicating he understands because he doesn't fully realize what's happening.

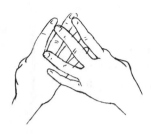

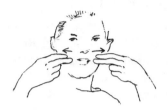

*Jail. With both hands in "4" shapes, bring the back of your right hand against the palm of your left hand several times. The fingers indicate the bars of a jail cell.*

*Thief. With both hands in "H" shapes and palms facing down, start with your fingertips under your nose and move your hands apart, toward your shoulders. This indicates the mustache of a bandit.*

*Steal. With your right hand in the bent "V" shape, fingers pointed left and your palm down, move your hand from your bent, left elbow toward your wrist, pulling your fingers up into a "claw" shape as you go. This indicates the motion of taking something away.*

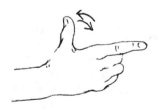

*Kill. Jab the extended index finger of your right hand (palm down) downward and under your left hand, which is open with the palm down. This indicates the motion of stabbing someone.*

*Gun. With your right hand in the "L" shape, index finger pointed forward with your palm front, move your thumb as though pulling a trigger. This indicates the motion of firing a gun.*

# Somebody Call My Lawyer

We've already discussed the problems sometimes encountered by Deaf people who find themselves within the legal or justice system.

**Signposts**
Like any potential juror, a Deaf person can be rejected as a jury member for a variety of reasons. What Deaf people are saying is that they shouldn't be rejected just because they are Deaf.

Another problem is that it's often difficult for Deaf people who wish to do so to get involved with the justice system because Deaf people are seldom called for jury duty. Many states do not even include the names of Deaf people in the lists of those residents eligible for jury duty.

Groups of Deaf people, in their ongoing efforts to gain access to all the rights and responsibilities of our society, have organized efforts to change the jury situation. Thanks to their work, some Deaf people have been called as jurors and been provided with interpreters.

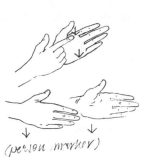

*(person marker)*

*Lawyer. With your right hand in the "L" shape, touch it to the top of the open palm of your left hand, which faces right, and slide it down to the bottom of the palm. Add the person marker. This is an initialized sign for "law," plus the person marker.*

*Judge. With both hands in "F" shapes, held apart but facing each other, move in alternating motions up and down in front of your chest. Add the person marker. This indicates the scales that weigh justice.*

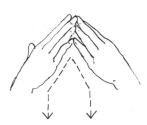

*Courthouse. Make the sign for "judge" (see previous illustration), and then the sign for "house" by touching the fingertips of your open hand together, then moving them down at an angle. The hand movement in "house" indicates the shape of the roof on a building.*

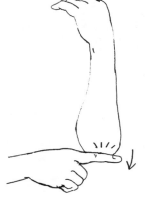

*Punishment. With your right index finger extended, hit it sharply against your left elbow. This indicates striking, as in punishment.*

# The Least You Need to Know

➤ The legal system can be very intimidating for Deaf people who have trouble communicating.

➤ Deaf people are entitled to interpreters in certain situations, but interpreters are often limited or not sufficiently qualified.

➤ Deaf people demanding their rights have caused the situation to begin to improve, but there's still a long way to go.

➤ Conditions for Deaf people are better in the United States than in many other countries.

➤ Deaf people have traditionally been excluded from serving as jurors.

# Come and Worship

Religion has had an important role in the history of Deaf people. Remember that it was Charles Michel de l'Epée, a French priest, who started the first school for Deaf children way back in the late 1760s.

In the United States, the first public school for the Deaf was founded by Thomas H. Gallaudet, a Protestant minister. Both de l'Epée and Gallaudet said the desire to instill religion in their young Deaf students was a primary motivator for starting the schools.

In this chapter, we'll learn about churches that are geared toward Deaf people, as well as some criticisms the Deaf have concerning some of those churches. We'll also learn some signs for things associated with religion.

# Thank You for Your Support

Gallaudet found financial support for his school from New England Protestants, who believed education was necessary to save the souls of these unenlightened children.

About 30 years after Gallaudet founded his school in New England, his son started the country's first congregation for Deaf people in New York City. Soon after, a second congregation was formed in Philadelphia, led by the Rev. Henry Syle, the nation's first ordained Deaf priest.

The Episcopal church led the way, but other denominations followed suit. There was a great deal of growth among Deaf churches and the number of Deaf ministers in the first part of the 1900s. Experts say this is because the ministry was one of the few professions that was open to Deaf people.

Deaf churches have played active roles in the Deaf community. Some have established schools and camps for young people, homes for elderly Deaf people, and services for Deaf people and their families.

Trinity Lutheran Church in Reading, Pennsylvania, offers worship services, prayer groups, and Bible classes in ASL. But, as is the case with many Deaf churches, Trinity has become much more to its members than a place to worship.

There are signing classes for parents and grandparents, and groups in which caregivers can voice concerns and seek advice about their children's education, socialization, and health. There are youth programs for kids, and multigenerational groups in which older church members serve as role models and mentors for younger ones. There are *pizza with a purpose* nights, field trips, sleepovers, and summer Bible schools and hayrides.

### Sign of the Times

Trinity Lutheran Church in Reading, Pennsylvania, has served the area's Deaf population for 85 years. In the early 1900s, a pastor traveled 50 miles from Philadelphia to conduct services in sign language. The church got its own pastor during the 1920s, and has operated continuously since then as a church for Deaf congregations.

Some members of Deaf culture, however, are frustrated because even churches with Deaf congregations have traditionally been run by hearing people. Critics say these church leaders have not done their share in promoting the rights of Deaf people, and have not created churches that reflect the concerns and culture of Deaf members.

218

Members of Deaf culture are striving to attain leadership of their own churches, and have enjoyed much progress during the past few years. As recognition and respect for Deaf people increases in other areas, they are growing in matters related to religion as well.

# Where We Go to Pray

Regardless if it's a synagogue, mosque, chapel, or a quiet spot on a mountaintop, the places where we worship are important to us. These are places where we should feel safe and welcomed—a haven from the confusion and haste of everyday life.

*Pray. Press your palms together as if praying, then move them together in small circles.*

*Religion. With your right hand in the "R" shape, start your fingertips on your chest at your heart or on your shoulder, with your palm facing your body. Move your hand down and out until your palm is turned down and your fingers are extended outward. This is an initialized sign indicating feelings coming from your heart.*

*Church. With your right hand in the "C" shape and your left hand in the "S" shape, tap the thumb side of your right hand on the back of your left hand. This is an initialized sign indicating a church built on a rock.*

+ person marker

*Temple. With your right hand in the "T" shape and your left hand in the "S" shape, tap the heel of your right hand on the back of your left hand. This is an initialized sign, similar to that for "church."*

*Minister. With your right hand in the "F" shape, start at the side of your face with your palm turned outward. Move your hand forward a couple of times with small, jerky motions. Add the person marker. This is the sign for "preach" and the person marker; the sign for "preach" indicates giving information or advice.*

*Commandments. With your right hand in the "C" shape and your palm facing out, touch it twice to your left, open palm.*

# Spirituality

**Signposts**
ASL signs for things associated with religion may vary depending on where they originated. For instance, there are several signs for "Buddha," but they're not standardized. We recommend that "Buddha" be finger spelled.

Spirituality, the quality that some believe most sets humans apart from animals, has factored into sign language ever since de l'Epée used it to teach religion to Deaf people in Paris and the surrounding areas.

Spirituality comes in all forms, some of which are not always compatible with others. We all know of the great wars fought, and still being fought, in the name of religion.

Despite the great differences among all the religions of the world, however, nearly all of them concur on the idea of a higher or divine being that serves as the focus for our spiritualism.

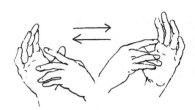

*God. Move your open right hand, palm facing left, in a downward, arcing motion from above your head to your face. This indicates a hand coming down from heaven.*

*Jesus. With your right hand in the "5" shape, touch your bent, middle finger into the middle of your left palm, which is held up and faces your right palm. Then reverse the movement, touching your right palm with your left finger. This indicates the nail holes made in the hands of Jesus when he was crucified.*

*Heaven. With both hands open, palms up and held up at either side of your head, move them up and out in a wavy motion, ending with your hands together, over your head. This indicates moving into the clouds.*

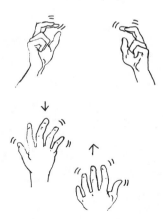

*Hell. With both hands in "3" shapes and your thumbs on your temples, bend your index and middle fingers up and down several times. Then, with both hands in "5" shapes, wiggle your fingers and move your hands up and down in alternating movements. This is the sign for "devil," then the sign for "fire."*

**221**

*Bible. Make the sign for "Jesus" (see earlier illustration), followed by the sign for "book." To make the sign for "book," put the palms of both hands together in front of you with your fingers pointing forward. Bring your palms apart, while keeping your little fingers touching. This indicates the "book of Jesus."*

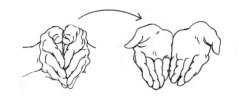

*Torah. Starting with both hands in "S" shapes and held in front of you at waist level, palms facing each other, move your hands away from each other by twisting your wrists up and down. This indicates the motion of unrolling a scroll.*

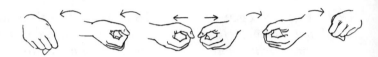

*Holy. With your right hand in the "H" shape and your palm facing your body, move it down over your upturned left hand, opening your right fingers into an open hand as you brush across the left fingertips. This is an initialized sign, made like the sign for "clean."*

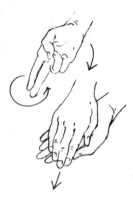

*Sin. With the index fingers of both hands extended and palms facing each other, move your hands together in small circles in front of your body.*

# All God's Children

God's children come in many colors and live in different parts of the world. Some hear, some do not. Some see, others don't. Some run, others can't walk. And they call themselves many different things. Next we'll show you a sign for some of the world's major religions. There are signs for the major religions of the world, but they vary greatly, and some are finger spelled.

**Signposts**
The names for some religious groups are initialized and then finger spelled in ASL. An example is "L-D-S" for Latter Day Saints.

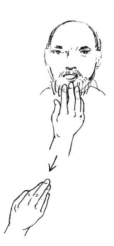

*Jewish. With your right hand in the "5" shape, start with your fingertips on your chin and move them downward, closing your fingers in toward your thumb as you go. Repeat the motion. This indicates the shape of a beard on a traditional Jewish man.*

For the term "Christian," make the sign for "Jesus" (see earlier illustration), then add the person marker.

For the term "Buddhist," as with "Buddah," we recommend that you finger spell this one. Don't forget to add the person marker.

# The Least You Need to Know

➤ Religion has a strong role in the history of signed languages and in ASL in particular.

➤ Deaf churches and ministries grew rapidly in the early 1900s.

➤ Churches are often much more to Deaf people than places to pray.

➤ Members of Deaf culture are working for greater autonomy within their churches.

➤ Many signs associated with religion are initialized or iconic.

# Part 5
# Fine-Tuning

*We've covered a lot of signs, but our work isn't finished yet. If grammar wasn't your favorite topic in high school, please accept our apologies. In this section, we're going to get a quick American Sign Language grammar lesson, as well as look at some of the subtle and intricate qualities of the language.*

*We'll also talk about opportunities for using ASL, continuing your ASL education, and some of the humor found in the language. So, stick around, there's still a lot to learn.*

# We're Not Done Yet!

Now that you've learned many different signs, you're probably anxious to get out there and start using them. Well, hold on just one minute—not so fast there. We've got a little fine-tuning to do.

Some of us might want to forget those high school grammar classes we sat through, with their discussions of objects, subjects, indirect objects, modifiers, and so on. There's no denying, however, that grammar is vitally important to a language, whether signed or spoken. All languages have rules of grammar that give them structure and make them understandable.

In this chapter we'll look at some basic points of grammar in ASL. There are numerous books available that go into great detail about the grammar of ASL, and if you're going to be very involved with using the language, it would be a good idea to check them out. For now, though, we'll take you through a quick course.

# Word Order: Is It a Tall Tree or a Tree Tall?

Since we talked about the placement of adjectives in Chapter 21, we'll just give you a little refresher here.

Adjectives in ASL normally come after the words they describe. For example, for "tall tree" you would sign "tree" and then "tall." But when a noun is used as an adjective, like "Christmas tree," the adjective comes before the word it's describing.

There is more involved with word order in ASL, however, than where you sign an adjective in relationship to a noun.

Word order is very important in English and in other languages such as Vietnamese and Mandarin Chinese. It helps us to see the role of a particular word in a sentence. In some languages, though, like Russian or Latin, word order is rather incidental.

Russian and Latin, a well as other languages like Finnish, Greek, and Swahili, rely more on grammatical tools to indicate the roles of words within a sentence then on how those words are placed within the sentence.

ASL uses word order and grammatical tools to establish the roles or words within a sentence. Although it has a basic sentence structure of object - subject - verb, it also changes the form of some signs to show grammatical relationship of signs within a sentence.

Signs for a class of verbs called *directional verbs* are prime examples of this. Consider the verb *help*. By using the same sign, but changing the direction in which it moves, the person signing can convey:

➤ I help you

➤ You help me

➤ You help her

➤ He helps me

➤ She helps you

There are many of these directional verbs, and they're important in establishing what's going on in an ASL sentence. If the signer signs "help" away from himself and toward the person he's signing to, he's indicating "I help you." If he signs it away from the person he's signing to and toward himself, he's indicating "you help me."

To indicate "he helps me," the signer would make the sign away from the person he's referring to and toward himself. If the person he's referring to is not present, the signer would designate a spot to represent the person, and make the sign moving away from that spot, and toward himself. Designating a spot to represent a person not present is called *indexing*, and was discussed in Chapter 7. The spot that's been designated becomes the spatial location from which the verb can be signed.

The concept of directional verbs is easy. You just move your hands in the direction in which whatever you're signing about is moving. If help is coming toward you, the sign moves toward you. If it's going from *him* to *her*, the movement of the sign follows that route.

> **A Good Sign**
> Grammatical aspects of ASL require careful attention from beginning signers. Eventually, though, you'll incorporate them into your signing without even thinking about it.

Most languages make use of both word order and grammatical tools to indicate the roles of words within a sentence. ASL is no exception.

# Not! Using Negatives in ASL

There are several ways to signify something negative in ASL. The first is very simple. Simply shake your head *no* as you sign. This form of negation is acquired very early by children learning to sign.

A second way is to add the sign for "not" to whatever you're signing. Simply sign "not" and then "happy" to indicate that someone is sad. Of course, "sad" has its own sign, so often you'll have a choice.

Other signs are made negative by twisting the wrist outward. For example, to sign "don't know," you'd tap the fingertips of your right hand to your temple, which is the sign for "know." Then, you'd turn your wrist outward in a twisting motion, changing the meaning of the sign to "don't know."

> **A Good Sign**
> If your friend asks you to help move a sofa, and you can't do it because you hurt your back, your facial expression will indicate regret when you tell your buddy you can't help. But, your facial expression would be quite different if you're very angry with someone and telling him you won't do something. Facial expression can't be stressed too much as an important part of ASL.

Facial expression is very important when expressing negation in ASL. It can, along with shaking of the head, indicate anger, sorrow, pity, or dismay. Don't forget about it!

# Pronouns: Is Everyone Accounted for?

We talked about establishing location to indicate possession in Chapter 7, and the use of spatial location was mentioned earlier in this chapter. This practice of establishing location is also used to indicate pronouns such as "I," "me," "he," "him," "she," "her," "you," "we," "us," "they," "them," and "those."

If the person about whom the signer is signing is present, the signer simply points at the person. If the person is not present, the signer establishes a spatial marker to stand in for the person.

Typically, the signer will finger spell the person's name, or give his sign name while pointing to a particular spot. The assigned spot is usually on the signer's non-dominant side. From then on in the conversation, that spot will "stand in" for Bobby whenever the signer refers to him.

Some pronouns, like those listed below, do have signs. Indexing, however, is common and must be understood in order to sign and understand signing effectively.

*Myself. With your right hand in the "A" shape, tap the thumb side of your hand to the center of your chest. This is an indexing sign; change your hand position to indicate pronouns such as "himself," "herself," or "yourself."*

*My. With your right hand in the closed "5" shape, lay it on the center of your chest. To emphasize "my," tap your hand on your chest.*

*You. Point your right extended index finger forward at the person to whom you're referring. To indicate a plural "you," point at several spots or move your finger back and forth in front of your body.*

*We. With your right index finger extended, move it in a circular motion from your right shoulder to your left shoulder with your palm facing your body.*

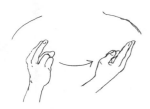

*Us. With your right hand in the "U" shape and your palm facing left, move your hand in a circular motion across your body, turning it until your palm faces left.*

*Our. With your right hand in the open palm shape, palm facing left, curve your hand and arm around in front of your body until your palm faces right.*

*Those. Point to the objects or people to which you are referring.*

*Your. Face your open right hand straight ahead with the palm out. This sign is the opposite of "my" or "mine;" signed with the palm out instead of in.*

*Yours, theirs, hers, his. With your right hand in the open palm shape, move it out slightly, away from your body. This is a type of indexing sign; its meaning should be made clear by the context in which it's used.*

*Someone, something. With your right index finger extended and your palm facing your body, move your hand back and forth repeatedly in a left-to-right motion. The context of the conversation will indicate whether the "someone" or "something" sign is being used.*

**231**

*Thing. With your right hand in the open palm shape and your palm up, move it in an arc from the center of your body to the right of your body.*

*Nothing. With your right hand in the "S" shape, start with it under your chin, then move it down and out while opening your fingers.*

*Here. With both your hands in the open palm shapes and palms up, move them in small circles in front of your chest.*

*There. Point your index finger at a specific place or point outward with your hand in an open palm shape.*

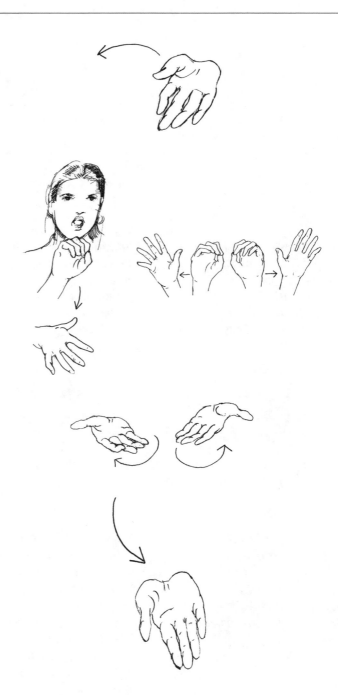

# Prepositions and Conjunctions

Before we begin to discuss prepositions and conjunctions in relationship to ASL, let's briefly review how they relate to English.

Prepositions, for those who may have forgotten, are words that show position or relation of one thing to another, like "under," "over," "on," "above," and "in." Conjunctions are "joining" words, such as "and," "but," and "or." Remember those? There is a sign for "or," but the preferred way is to finger spell "O-R."

Prepositions and conjunctions are used in ASL, but nowhere to the extent that they are in English. Prepositions are used when signing is being done in English order, but they are usually replaced by *directional signing*, which indicates position or relation of one thing to another without use of these bothersome little words.

Incorporating meaning into signs is a skill that comes naturally to good, experienced signers, and it's one of the things that makes ASL such a streamlined and efficient language.

> **Signposts**
> Some signs for prepositions are basically the same, but use different location of the dominant hand. For instance, the signs for "above" and "below" are the same handshape and movement, but the location of the dominant hand changes. They're opposite signs, as words have opposite meanings.

Having said all that, we're going to show you some prepositions and conjunctions. You'll use these as you're learning ASL, but you should find they become less important as you learn to incorporate them in your signing.

There are enough prepositions and conjunctions to get you started, but don't forget—the goal is to move past them and be able to convey your thought with directional signing.

*In. With the fingertips of your right hand touching your right thumb, put them down into your left hand, which is in the "C" shape. This indicates putting something into something else.*

233

Out. Start with your right hand open, inserted with the fingers pointed down into your left "C" hand. Bring your right hand out of your left, closing your right thumb and fingers as your hand moves upward. This indicates taking some-thing out of something else, such as cookies from a cookie jar.

Behind. With both hands in "A" shapes and held together, your palms facing each other and the thumbs extended, move your right hand backward toward your body. This indicates something moving from behind something else.

Between. With both hands in open palm shapes, insert your right hand between the index finger and thumb of your left hand and rock your right hand back and forth. This indicates something that is between other objects.

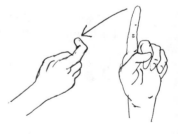

Above. With both hands in open palm shapes, circle your right hand above the left. This indicates something above something else.

Below. With both hands in open palm shapes, circle your left hand above the right. This indicates one object moving below another; this sign is opposite of the sign for "above."

From. Start with your right index finger (right hand in the "X" shape) touching the upward extended index finger of your left hand. Then move your right hand to the right. This indicates taking something away from something else.

*And. Start with your right hand in front of you, fingers spread apart and facing down. Then, draw your hand to the right while pulling your finger-tips together.*

*But. Cross your index fingers, with your palms facing out. Then, draw your fingers apart.*

*Because. Start with your right index finger at the right side of your forehead, then bring it out in a slight arc, closing your hand into the "A" shape. A common variation on this sign is to start with your right hand in the closed "5" shape and proceed as mentioned.*

# The Least You Need to Know

➤ Word order is secondary in importance to inflections in ASL.

➤ There are several ways to express negatives in ASL.

➤ Indexing is important when indicating pronouns, although there are signs for some pronouns.

➤ Prepositions and conjunctions are used less often in ASL than in English.

➤ Experienced signers often use directional signing instead of signs for prepositions and conjunctions.

(?)

# Chapter 25

# Ask Me a Question

## In This Chapter

➤ Finding that rhetorical questions have their place

➤ Signing *yes/no* questions

➤ Signing *who/what/when/where/why/and how* questions

➤ Using facial expression when asking questions

Regardless of the language you're using, there will always be a need for questions. Think about how many questions you ask in the course of an average day. "Are you ready to go?" "Did you have enough soup?" "What time does the show start?" "Are we going to take a walk tonight?"

People are generally an inquisitive bunch, whether their language is spoken or signed. In this chapter, we'll learn how questions in ASL are divided into two main groups, and the role of rhetorical questions. We'll also learn some signs for words associated with questions.

# Could You Repeat the Question?

There are two basic categories of questions in ASL. One is the *yes/no* category, and the other is the *who/what/when/where/why/ and how* category.

As you would imagine, the *yes/no* category includes all those questions that can be answered with either a *yes* or a *no*.

"Did it rain last night?" "Are you getting a haircut today?" "Is your brother still in the hospital?" "Will you have a cake for your birthday?" "Did you remember to take out the trash?" You know, those kinds of questions. Sure, there might be an occasional "maybe," but these questions are pretty much to the point.

The other category is all the questions that require a bit more information, such as, "Who is the woman you were having dinner with last night?" "What happened that made you three hours late for your appointment?" "When are you going on vacation?" "Where did you buy that suit?" "Why didn't you take out the trash?" "How will you get to Florida?"

There are other words and phrases, such as *which*, *how many*, and *what's up* that could fit in this category, but the ones mentioned previously are the most used.

Actually, there's a third type of question in ASL, but it's not a true question form. Rhetorical questions, as in English, are questions that are asked but that don't really require an answer. They are valuable because they provide a means for the signer to set the stage for whatever information will follow.

We've all used rhetorical questions. Something like, "Wow, look at the mess I've made. How the heck did that happen?" Or, "I can't find my shoes. Where did I put those things?" Sometimes they're pointless because nobody knows what we're talking (or signing) about. Sometimes, though, they serve as tools in our conversations. Signers use rhetorical questions quite frequently; much more often, studies show, than people who speak.

This frequent use of rhetorical questions might just be a quirk of Deaf culture, sort of like the need to tell a story from beginning to end that we discussed in Chapter 22. Or, some experts say, rhetorical questions, when used in signing, let it be known that the information to follow is important.

The signer asks a question and then supplies the answer himself as a means of conveying information.

# Is That a Yes or a No?

We'll get back to asking questions in the next section, but first we'll tell you how to answer a question in the *yes/no* category. We've added *maybe*, because nobody can be decisive all the time.

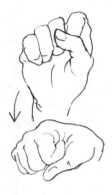

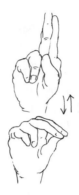

*Yes. With your right hand in the "S" shape, move it up and down repeatedly by bending your wrist. This indicates a head nodding yes.*

*No. With your right index and middle fingers extended, close them to your thumb and repeat the motion.*

*Maybe. With both hands in closed "5" shapes and palms up, start with your right hand low and your left hand high. Then move your right hand up and your left hand down, and then back to their original positions.*

# Who, What, When, Where, Why, and How?

The signed equivalent of a question mark, shown in the following illustration, can be added to the beginning or the end of a question. Additionally, the question word (who, what, when, etc.) is often signed at both the beginning and the end of the question.

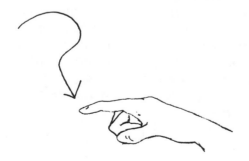

*Question. Using your extended right index finger, draw the shape of a question mark in the air. Start with your index finger pointed up and your palm out, and end with your palm down and your finger pointed out.*

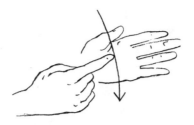

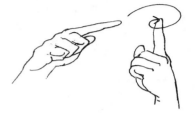

*Who. With your right index finger extended and your palm facing in, draw a small circle around your mouth. This indicates the shape of the mouth when saying "who"; there are also other common ways of signing "who."*

*What. With the index finger of your right hand extended, draw it down over your left, open palm.*

*When. With both hands in "1" shapes, your right palm facing down and your left palm up, use your right index finger to make a half circle over your left index finger. Then touch the tips of both index fingers together.*

*Where. With your right index finger extended and your palm facing forward, shake your finger back and forth. This is the natural expression of questioning "where."*

*Why. Start with the fingertips of your bent right hand on your forehead, your palm toward your face. Move your hand away from your head in a downward motion, changing it into the "Y" shape as it moves. This indicates removing something from your brain to analyze it.*

*How. Start with both hands in front of your chest, your palms in and the backs of your knuckles pressed together. Then roll your hands over, in an upward motion, until your palms are facing up and the backs of your fingers are together.*

# Let Your Face Ask the Question

No matter what kind of question you're asking—*yes/no, who/what/when/why/where/or how* or rhetorical, it won't be correct if you don't use the proper facial expressions.

When asking a *yes/no* question, it's proper to lean forward and raise your eyebrows as you're signing. You should open your eyes wide and look at the person to whom you're signing.

For a *who/what/when/why/where/or how* question, you should furrow your eyebrows and lean forward. Sometimes the shoulders are raised, and the head is often tilted to one side. People who don't understand the facial expressions and body language used in ASL often think a signer is angry when he makes the appropriate expression for a who, what, etc. question.

Although rhetorical questions are not true questions, they too should be accompanied by proper facial expression. Raising the eyebrows and tilting the head to one side are correct actions when asking a rhetorical question.

Don't assume that drawing the *question mark* gets you off the hook for facial expression. It is still important, even when you're manually expressing a question.

# The Least You Need to Know

➤ There are two basic types of questions in ASL.

➤ Rhetorical questions aren't true questions, but they serve a valuable purpose.

➤ There is a signed equivalent to the written question mark that can be used to indicate a question.

➤ Facial expression is extremely important when signing questions.

➤ Different types of questions require different facial expressions.

# Use It or Lose It

By now, you should have a basic knowledge of ASL. You're by no means an expert—remember that little lecture from Chapter 4—but hopefully you've at least gotten an understanding of the language. We hope too, that you've learned something about the history of Deaf people, of Deaf culture, and about education for the Deaf.

As with many minority groups, Deaf people have had to struggle for rights and opportunities. While they've made great strides, there is still much work to do. We hope this book will have increased your sensitivity to issues affecting Deaf people and made you more aware of the hurdles they've faced and continue to face every day.

In this wrap-up chapter, we'll talk about ways to practice and increase your knowledge of ASL. We'll also review some of the intricacies of the language, tell you a little bit about the humor found in ASL, and talk about ASL as a two-way language.

# Can You Relate?

One of the best ways we can think of to help you understand how Deaf people struggle and why they develop such deep bonds with one another is to ask you to imagine the following scenario.

You've moved to Japan because your spouse was transferred there for business. You don't know anybody there except your spouse, and soon after you arrive he or she is moved temporarily to another part of the country to complete a job. You're left alone. You don't know one word of Japanese and the people around you speak no English. You do the best you can to communicate, but every day is a struggle. You find it extremely difficult to buy groceries, ask for directions, or do any of the things you've always taken for granted.

> **Warning Sign**
> After reading this book, you hopefully have acquired some insights into Deaf culture about which most people have no awareness. But please don't assume you know how Deaf people feel or think. First, there are many different opinions within the Deaf community, as there are within any community. Also, we've taken a glimpse of Deaf culture in this book. Deaf people feel that only someone who was born Deaf can ever be a true part of Deaf culture.

One day, out of the blue, another American moves into the house next door. You're both alone, with extremely limited ability to communicate. You immediately bond with one another, sharing everything that happens. You spend as much time together as possible, hating to leave the security of being able to understand and be understood.

If you can truly imagine and try to understand this scenario, it will give you a glimpse into the isolation Deaf people experience every day, and why socialization with other Deaf people is so important.

# Opportunities for Using ASL

Now that you've acquired some knowledge about ASL, what will you do with it? We hope you won't stash it away someplace, never to be used again, like those courses you took on lugeing in Bangladesh and 16th-century French literature.

Because ASL is a living, growing language used by more people every day, you're going to run into it again, whether you're looking for it or not.

You've worked hard to learn the signs for the manual alphabet, numbers, and some words, so go ahead and try them out. If you have a Deaf friend or relative—lucky you! Hopefully, he or she will be happy that you're learning ASL and will take the time to work with you. If you don't know someone who's Deaf, you'll have to be a bit creative.

We discussed some opportunities for using ASL in Chapter 4, and you might want to review that to refresh your memory.

Social service agencies that provide services for Deaf people often operate on tight budgets and would welcome volunteers. You could provide a valuable service while getting the chance to practice signing. If there is a school for the Deaf in your area, you may be able to volunteer there. How about theater productions for the Deaf? Wouldn't it be interesting to watch a play performed in sign language?

**Signposts**
Some organizations that offer services, products or information for Deaf people, and hearing people interested in ASL, deafness and issues concerning Deaf people, are named in Appendix A of this book.

If you know a Deaf person who is willing to introduce you to his or her Deaf friends and take you along to some social events, you're very lucky. You're sure to enjoy the lively signing and you'll get a taste of Deaf culture. A really great experience, if you live close enough, would be to visit Gallaudet University in Washington, D.C. The energy at the university is tremendous, and it's an exciting, lively place to watch (and maybe even participate in) some ASL.

If you're interested in learning more about sign language, your next step is to enroll in a class. Look for these locally—they're often offered at schools, community centers, or community colleges. But be sure to get some information about the instructor who will be teaching the class. There are no required standards for sign language teachers. For whatever reasons, people sometimes feel they're qualified to teach when they're barely more than beginners themselves.

The best sign language teachers, with a few exceptions, are Deaf. This isn't to say a hearing person can't be a good teacher, but the best teachers generally are those who live with the language.

# Appreciating the Eloquence and Intricacies

We hope by now you've developed an appreciation for the eloquence and intricacies of ASL. We also hope you've begun to understand how much fun this language is.

Full of subtleties and nuances, a turn of the hand or a shake of the head can change the meaning of a sign. A facial expression can quickly turn a positive into a negative, the direction of a sign can change its meaning, and the speed of a moving finger can indicate languor or haste.

Consider the sign for "give." With both hands in the flat "O" shape moving away from your body, you're giving something to someone else. Turn your hands around and move them toward you, however, and somebody is giving something to you. It's purely directional.

Some of the intricacies and eloquences are hard to pick up on if you don't use ASL all the time. Signs over time tend to change. They become easier. Excessive motions are eliminated. The signs are made streamlined. It's like contractions in English, or like the phrase that kids often use when they show up at their friends' house around dinnertime: "J'eat yet?" Which translates to, "Did you eat yet?"

How about two office workers discussing a problem, when one excuses himself. "Hold on, I wanna cuppa coffee," he says. Which translates to, "Hold on, I want a cup of coffee."

Signing is no different. There are shortcuts and subtleties that someone who hasn't known and used the language for a long time won't be able to understand. As you use the language, you'll discover and appreciate more and more of these subtleties.

# Funny Stuff

Did you hear the one about the Deaf man and his wife who were out for a drive on a warm spring day? They got to the railroad tracks and stopped as the crossing gates came down. They watched the train pass, then waited for the gates to be raised. And waited…and waited…

Finally, the wife noticed the man in charge of raising and lowering the gates was asleep in the control tower. She told her husband to write a note, telling the man to raise the gates. The husband did, and he took the note to the man in the tower.

He came down and told his wife the man was awake and had the note. Still, the gates weren't raised. By this time the man was very angry. "What did you write on the note?" his wife asked. "I asked him to please but the gate," said the husband.

"But" the gate!? The joke is that the sign for "but" is the same as the gesture for "Open the gates." The Deaf man told the gatekeeper to "but" the gate.

This is an example of humor in ASL. ASL is filled with funny stuff. There are jokes, plays on signs, puns, all kind of things. This joke, though, is also an example of how humor often doesn't translate well from culture to culture.

Consider this example of a hearing joke.

### Signs of the Times

Linguists say it is significant that users of ASL employ humor and play with their language as users of other languages do. It is another argument that ASL is indeed a true language, with rules that can be broken for artistic effect by those who understand them.

A cornflake was at the very bottom of the box. He dearly wanted to be top cornflake, so he clawed and climbed his way to the top of the box. Soon after, an old woman turned the box upside down and the cornflake fell to the bottom.

He clawed and climbed his way to the top again. Soon after, an old woman turned the box upside down and the cornflake fell to the bottom.

He clawed and climbed his way to the top again. Soon after, an old woman turned the box upside down and the cornflake fell to the bottom.

He clawed and climbed his way to the top again. Soon after, an old woman turned the box upside down and the cornflake fell to the bottom.

(Eventually, the person hearing the joke gets tired of the repetition and tells the person telling the joke to get to the punch line.)

"There is no punch line," the person telling the joke says. "It's a serial."

Serial—cereal. Get it? Well, a Deaf person wouldn't get it because he wouldn't know that "serial" and "cereal" sound the same. Most jokes aren't universal. It is reputed that on the floor of the United Nations, translators don't even attempt to translate jokes. Supposedly, most of the hundreds of translators on the floor will tell the people for whom they're translating that the speaker is telling a joke and those listening should laugh when he's done.

There is a humorous, true story that has become fairly widespread among Deaf people.

A math teacher was sent to Gallaudet University to teach a class. He knew no sign language. He hated using an interpreter in his class and decided he would learn to sign. So he started hanging out in the cafeteria between classes, signing and watching others sign. Soon he became more comfortable with ASL and started using it sometimes in his class.

> **A Good Sign**
> Proficient signers enjoy making the equivalent of spoken puns or plays on words. An example is the colloquial sign for "bar hopping." The left fingers are held apart to indicate "bars," while the right fingers "hop" from one "bar" to another.

One day he came to class particularly animated. He signed to his students that he was very, very tired. "I've been working all morning with my secretary," was what he intended to sign. Unfortunately, his signing wasn't as good as he thought and he signed "I've been necking all morning with my secretary."

Of course, the signs for "working" and "necking" are similar, so this is a feasible mistake for a beginning signer. This sort of humor appeals to Deaf and hearing people, but some, clearly, does not.

# Receiving Sign Language

It might be true that it's better to give than to receive, but remember that in ASL it's a two-way street. ASL is a conversational language, and conversation means more than one person. Receiving signs is a vital part of ASL, so pay close attention to the one who is signing to you.

Remember the rules about watching the person who is signing at all times, and pay particular attention to facial expression and body language. Soon you'll be receiving sign language without even thinking about it.

# A Closing Sign

We hope you've enjoyed your beginning journey into American Sign Language, and we wish you luck as you continue your journey. We'll leave you with one more sign—the one that has become something of a hallmark for ASL.

Pay attention to this one. It may very well be the most important sign you'll ever perform—or receive.

*I love you. With your right hand in the "I love you" handshape, hold it in front of your chest. The "I love you" handshape is upright, palm out, with the middle and index finger bent down.*

# The Least You Need to Know

➤ Hearing people can try, but never fully understand the isolation and difficulties experienced by Deaf people.

➤ It's important to find places and people with whom you can use and practice ASL.

➤ A class with a qualified ASL instructor is your next step if you're going to continue learning ASL.

➤ Remember to keep an eye open for the subtleties of ASL.

➤ There is abundant humor in ASL. But keep in mind that many jokes do not have cross-cultural appeal.

➤ You've got to be receptive to receiving signs because ASL is a two-way language.

# Resources for the Deaf and for Families and Friends

There is a growing number of resources supporting Deaf people and their families and friends. Such resources offer human services, youth programs, educational opportunities, information on programs and conferences, guidance on health and hearing issues, support groups, and other things of interest.

Below is a sampling of some of the organizations and resources available.

## Better Hearing Institute

This organization provides information on deafness, deafness in children, and other topics. It can be accessed at its Web site at http://www.betterhearing.org/.

## Children of Deaf Adults

c/o Texas School for the Deaf
P.O. Box 3538
Austin, TX 78764
512-440-5300

This group offers support and services for children of deaf adults.

## DEAFPRIDE

1350 Potomac Avenue SE
Washington, D.C. 20003
202-675-6700 (Voice/TTY)

This is a nonprofit advocacy that works on behalf of Deaf people and their families.

# DeafWorldWeb

This extensive Web site, featuring an ASL Dictionary Online, Products and Services, an E-Mail Directory, Deaf World News, and more, can be accessed at http:dww.deafworldweb.org.

# Gallaudet Research Institute

800 Florida Avenue NE
Washington, D.C. 20002
800-451-8834 or 202-651-5400

This organization conducts long-term research projects and supports the research projects of Gallaudet University faculty and staff.

# Hear Now

4001 S. Magnolia Way, Suite 100
Denver, CO 80237
800-648-HEAR (Voice/TTY)

This organization offers financial assistance to eligible persons.

# International Association of Parents of the Deaf

814 Thayer Avenue
Silver Spring, MD 20910
301-585-5400 (Voice/TTY)

The group offers support, education, and programs for parents of Deaf children.

# Junior NAD Newsletter

Junior National Association of the Deaf Branch Office
445 N. Pennsylvania Street, Suite 804
Indianapolis, IN 46204

This is a newsletter for young people who are members of Junior NAD. It is published four times per year.

# Junior National Association of the Deaf Youth Programs

445 N. Pennsylvania Street, Suite 804
Indianapolis, IN 46204
301-587-1788 (Voice/TTY)

This organization for Deaf youth offers an annual leadership camp, conferences, and various programs and resources.

# League for the Hard of Hearing

71 W. 23rd Street
New York, NY 10010-4162
212-741-7650 (Voice)
212-255-1932 (TTY)
212-255-4413 (Fax)

The League's Web site, which offers information, contacts, and a chat room, can be accessed at http://www/lhh.org/.

# NAD Broadcaster (Newsletter)

National Association of the Deaf
814 Thayer Avenue
Silver Spring, MD 20910

This is a Deaf community national newsletter, published 11 times a year by the National Association of the Deaf.

# National Association of the Deaf

814 Thayer Avenue
Silver Spring, MD 20910-4500
301-587-1789 (TTY)
301-587-1788 (Voice)
301-587-1791 (Fax)
*NADHQ@juno.com* (E-mail)

The National Association of the Deaf has an extensive Web site. It can be accessed at http://www.nad.org/nadhome.htm.

# National Center for Law and the Deaf

7th Street and Florida Avenue, NE
Washington, D.C. 20002
202-447-0445 (Voice and TTY)

This group provides legal support and education for Deaf people.

# Real World Success

215-256-0938 (Fax)
800-796-3323 (Voice)
800-855-2881 (TTY)

This group provides professional development and success motivation for Deaf and hard-of-hearing people. It can be reached on the Internet at www.realworldsuccess.com.

# National Information Center on Deafness

Gallaudet University
800 Florida Avenue NE
Washington, D.C. 20002
202-651-5051(Voice)
202-651-5052(TTY)

This center provides information and publications on a variety of subjects related to deafness.

# National Research Register for Heredity Hearing Loss

Boys Town National Research Hospital
555 30th Street
Omaha, NE 68154
402-498-6631 (Voice/TTY)

This hospital conducts genetic research, especially relating to hearing loss. It can be reached on the Internet at www.boystown.org/genetics.

# Registry of Interpreters for the Deaf, Inc.

511 Monroe Street, Suite 1107
Rockville, MD 20850
301-608-0050 (Voice/TTY)

This national organization, with chapters in every state, evaluates, trains, and places interpreters. It also advocates for interpreters in various situations involving Deaf people.

# Sunset International Bible Institute

This organization offers eight courses in Deaf communication, including ASL, and courses in interpreter training and Deaf psychology. It can be accessed on the Internet at http://www.hub.ofthe.net/sunset/deaf/htm.

Sunset representative Hollis Maynard can be reached at 806-795-8728.

# Telecommunications for the Deaf, Inc.

814 Thayer Avenue
Silver Spring, MD 20910
301-589-3786 (Voice)
301-589-3006 (TTY)

# The National Theatre of the Deaf

5 W. Main Street
Chester, CT 06412
860-526-4971 (Voice)
860-526-4974 (TTY)

This touring theatre, founded in 1967, presents plays using a combination of sign language and speech. It can be reached on the Internet at www.ntd.org.

# World Recreation Association of the Deaf, Inc./USA

P.O. Box 321
Quartz Hill, CA 93586
805-948-8879 (TTY)

This association promotes activities such as camping, skiing, and white-water rafting trips for Deaf people.

# Self Help for Hard of Hearing People, Inc.

7910 Woodmont Ave., Suite 1200
Bethesda, MD 20814
301-657-2249 (TTY)
301-657-2248 (Voice)

This organization offers a bimonthly magazine, extensive publications, annual conventions, and other services for hard-of-hearing people, their families, and friends. It provides education options and legislative updates and alerts. It can be reached on the Internet at www.shhh.org.

# National Technical Institute for the Deaf

Rochester Institute of Technology
National Technical Institute for the Deaf
Rochester, NY 14623-5604
716-475-6700 (TTY/Voice)
716-475-2696 (Fax)

One of seven colleges of Rochester (NY) Institute of Technology, this school offers undergraduate and graduate programs for qualified Deaf and hard-of-hearing students, as well as community resources and services. It can be reached on the Internet at www.rit.edu.NTID.

# "Did You Know That..."

➤ ...American Sign Language is a complete, visual-gestural language with its own grammar and vocabulary?

➤ ...ASL is *not* English translated in signs?

➤ ...ASL is the third-most-used language in the United States?

➤ ...babies in households where both ASL and spoken English are used often sign before they speak?

➤ ...ASL is recognized and accepted as a foreign language at many major universities, including Harvard, Brown, and Georgetown?

➤ ...Deaf culture is a real culture with traditions, idioms, stories, humor, poetry, and other art forms?

➤ ...Deaf people do not in any way consider themselves handicapped? (They are a minority, but not an impaired minority.)

➤ ...deafness is sometimes put into three categories: hard-of-hearing, severely deaf, and profoundly deaf?

➤ ...from March 6–11 in 1988, students at Gallaudet University in Washington, D.C. shut down the campus during a protest that resulted in the school's first Deaf president?

➤ ...the great majority of Deaf people marry other Deaf people and celebrate the birth of a Deaf child?

➤ ...Deaf children used to be punished—sometimes by having their hands tied down—for using sign language in school?

➤ ...in the mid-1800s there was a large population of Deaf people on Martha's Vineyard, Massachusetts, and nearly everyone on the island—Deaf and hearing—used sign language?

> ...the Deaf composer Ludwig van Beethoven carried blank notebooks for people to write messages to him? (More than 400 of these notebooks still survive.)

> ...about one million Deaf people use ASL as their primary, common language?

> ...ASL was greatly influenced by French sign language?

> ...the first American school for Deaf students was founded in Hartford, Connecticut, in 1917 by the Reverend Thomas Hopkins Gallaudet and Frenchman Laurent Clerc?

> ...Gallaudet University is the only liberal arts university especially for Deaf people in the world?

> ...many Deaf people use special devices, like flashing lights, to indicate the ringing of a telephone or doorbell?

> ...the parents of many Deaf children are told at one point that their child is learning disabled or mentally retarded?

> ...educational programs for Deaf students are primarily taught and overseen by hearing teachers and administrators?

> ...in some countries Deaf people are not permitted to get married?

> ...a Deaf child's first contact with Deaf culture often comes when he enters a Deaf school, and these schools very often remain extremely important to Deaf people for their entire lives?

> ...facial expression and body language is as important in ASL as the actual formation of signs?

> ...Deaf culture uses stories and storytelling as means of bonding and passing along wisdom and heritage?

# Glossary

The following are common terms relating to American Sign Language and Deaf culture.

**American Manual Alphabet**   A series of 26 handshapes that correspond to the letters of the English alphabet and are used for fingerspelling and as handshapes for American Sign Language.

**American Sign Language**   A visual-manual language that serves as the primary means of communication for a very large number of Deaf people in the United States and Canada.

**Autosomal Recessive Inheritance**   A condition in which a recessive gene for deafness is passed to a child by both parents. It is responsible for most hereditary deafness.

**Bonet, Juan Pablo** (1579–1623)   A Spaniard who in about 1620 wrote *Simplification of the Alphabet and the Art of Teaching Mutes to Speak*, the first published book of oral teaching methods for Deaf people.

**Clerc, Laurent** (1785–1869)   A Frenchman, deaf since the age of one, who helped Thomas Hopkins Gallaudet start the American School for the Deaf in 1916 in Hartford, Connecticut. A champion of the manual approach, Clerc is considered a hero by many Deaf people.

**Cochlear implant**   A device that is surgically implanted into the mastoid bone, designed to stimulate the hearing nerve and allow some degree of hearing. Cochlear implants are fiercely controversial among the Deaf community.

**CODA** (Child Of Deaf Adult)   Refers to a hearing child of at least one Deaf parent.

**Congenital deafness**   Deafness that occurs at or soon after birth. It is sometimes, but not always, caused by too little oxygen during a complicated labor and delivery.

**Cued speech**   A method of communication in which speechreading is accompanied by explanatory hand gestures to distinguish sounds that look alike on the lips.

**Deaf community**   A group of Deaf people who share common language, values, and experiences.

**Deaf culture**   The collective bonds, such as language, values, clubs, organizations, and attitudes that create a sense of unity and cohesiveness among Deaf people.

**Decibel**   A unit used to measure the intensity of sound, with zero decibels being the softest sound that can be heard by a person of normal hearing and 100 decibels being the loudest sound able to be produced by an audiometer.

**Dominant signing hand**   The hand that carries out the primary action of a sign. A right-handed person generally uses his right hand as his dominant signing hand. A left-handed person generally uses his left.

**l'Epée, Abbé Charles Michel de** (1712–1789)   A French priest who started the first school for Deaf children in France in the late 1750s or early 1760s. An early proponent of sign language, he became known as the founder of the manual approach.

**Fingerspelling**   The process of spelling out words using the American Manual Alphabet. It can be used on its own, but is very laborious. It is used in conjunction with American Sign Language to spell words for which there are no signs, like proper names and brand names.

**Gallaudet, Edward Miner** (1837–1917)   The son of Thomas Hopkins Gallaudet, Edward was the first superintendent of the Columbia Institution. He was a strong proponent of a dual educational system for Deaf students, combining oral methods with the manual approach.

**Gallaudet, Thomas Hopkins** (1787–1851)   Founded the American School for the Deaf in 1916 in Hartford, Connecticut, the first school for Deaf students in the United States. Gallaudet was a theologian, and the father of Edward Miner Gallaudet.

**Gallaudet University**   The world's only liberal arts university specifically for Deaf students. Located in Washington, D.C., it was founded in 1864 as the Columbia Institution for the Deaf and Dumb and Blind. It was renamed in 1894 to honor Thomas H. Gallaudet, who had founded the nation's first school for the Deaf.

**Genetic hearing loss**   The cause of a large percentage of hearing problems that occur at birth or in early childhood. There are about 200 different kinds of genetic hearing problems.

**Hand movement**   The direction and manner in which your hand or hands move when forming a sign. Hand movement is one of the four elements of a complete sign.

**Handshape**   The position of the fingers and palm when making a sign. Handshape is one of the four elements of a complete sign.

**Hard of hearing**   A term used to describe a lesser degree of hearing loss than the total loss that is deafness. *Hard of hearing* is preferred by the Deaf community over *hearing impaired.*

**Heinicke, Samuel** (1727–1790)   A German educator who in the late 1770s founded the first state-supported public school for Deaf students. Heinicke was a proponent of the oral approach.

**Iconic signs**   Also called *natural signs,* these are signs that resemble the objects they represent. Examples include "tea," "toothbrush," and "basketball."

**Initialized signs**   Signs that use the handshape of the first letter of the corresponding English word to distinguish themselves from other similar signs. Examples include "family," "team," and "group."

**Manual approach**   A method of communication among Deaf people that uses manual gestures (sign language). It is considered the natural means of communication for the Deaf.

**Modified signs**   Signs that have been intentionally changed in order to clarify their meanings. An example is changing the location of the sign for "zipper," to indicate where the zipper is located on the body.

**National Association of the Deaf (NAD)**   An advocacy organization for Deaf and hard-of-hearing people, based in Silver Spring, Maryland. The organization has 50 affiliated state associations and more than 22,000 members.

**Non-manual elements of signing**   Factors such as facial expression, body language, and eye contact that can change the meaning or intensity of a sign.

**Oral approach**   A method of communication that stresses the use of speech among Deaf people. Speech is usually combined with speechreading and auditory training, a combination which is thought by some to give Deaf people the tools they need to integrate with the hearing world.

**Otitus media**   An infection of the middle ear that is very common in children. If left untreated, it can result in hearing loss.

**Ototoxic drugs**   Drugs that can affect hearing by interfering with the function of the inner ear.

**Palm position**   The direction in which your palm or palms face when forming a sign. Palm position is one of the four elements of a complete sign.

**Pidgin Sign English**   A system of manual language that combines English word order with the vocabulary of American Sign Language. It is mostly used by hearing people who are learning to communicate with Deaf people.

**Presbycusis**   A type of sensorineural hearing loss that is a natural consequence of aging.

**Relay centers**   A telephone service that allows Deaf and hearing persons to communicate through a specially trained operator. The operator records a message from either a Deaf or hearing person, relays it to the other person, and then waits for a response.

**Residential school for the Deaf**   A boarding school for Deaf students. Many students favor residential schools because it is where they become fully immersed in Deaf culture.

**Sicard, Abbé Roch Ambroise Cucurron** (1742–1822)   This advocate of education for Deaf people trained under Abbé Charles Michel de l'Epée, and took over de l'Epée's school at the time of his death.

**Sign language interpreter**   Someone able to translate the meaning of spoken words into sign language as the words are spoken. Interpreting is a highly skilled job, requiring significant training.

**Sign-to-voice interpreter**   Someone able to translate the meaning of sign language into spoken language as it is being signed. Sign-to-voice was previously called *reverse interpreting*.

**Signing area**   The area in relationship to the body at which a sign is formed. Most signs are formed between the waist and the top of the head. This is one of the four areas of a complete sign.

**Signed English**   A manual system used to represent spoken English. Developed in 1973 by Gallaudet University educators, the system has 3,500 sign words and 14 sign markers that represent English words.

**Signing exact English**   A manual communication system commonly used in schools. It uses hand signs for words, prefixes, and endings, providing a clear, signed representation of English. It is often used in conjunction with spoken English in a total communication approach. The system was developed in 1972 by a Deaf woman, a mother of a Deaf child and a daughter of Deaf parents.

**Simultaneous communication**   A method of communication that combines the use of speech, speechreading, sign language, and fingerspelling. It is primarily used between Deaf and hearing people.

**SODA** (Sibling Of Deaf Adult)   Refers to a hearing person with at least one Deaf brother or sister.

**Speechreading**   A method of communication based on a Deaf person recognizing spoken words by watching the lips of the person speaking. Speechreading was taught in many schools for the Deaf as part of the oral method. It is also known as *lip reading*.

**Time line**   An imaginary line that passes through the body of the signer and is used to indicate time when signing. Time in the future is signed in front of the person, while time in the past is signed behind. The person's body represents present time.

**Total communication**   A philosophy of education that stresses exposure to and acceptance of all possible methods to help a Deaf person communicate. These could include sign language, speechreading, fingerspelling, speech, writing, and audio-visual methods. It was first developed in California by a teacher who had a Deaf child.

**Tinnitus**   Ringing in the ears that can indicate impending ear damage, especially if the person experiencing it is using a drug at the time.

**TTY machines**   Teletypewriters that are connected to telephone lines, allowing Deaf people to receive telephone messages and type messages back.

# Index

**267**

# E

# F

# G

## o

## P-Q